SUPER LOGIC
Modern Mathematics

SUPER LOGIC
Modern Mathematics

Classical Mathematics

Chong Kok Fah

PARTRIDGE

ISBN: Hardcover   978-1-4828-6567-7
          Softcover   978-1-4828-6566-0
          eBook   978-1-4828-6568-4

Print information available on the last page.

To order additional copies of this book, contact
Toll Free 800 101 2657 (Singapore)
Toll Free 1 800 81 7340 (Malaysia)
orders.singapore@partridgepublishing.com

www.partridgepublishing.com/singapore

Contents

Chapter 1

Arithmetic

Challenges of the Living Mathematics and Sciences

When humankind first had the desire to count, they had to invent the system of arithmetic to facilitate their counting needs. For instance, the leader of a group of four primitive tribespeople, upon returning from a hunting excursion in the woods, would assess the catch to make sure that he and his fellows had killed enough creatures – or collected enough fruits and vegetables – to satisfy the needs of his people. This practice led to the creation of basic arithmetic. Over time, new mathematic concepts were invented whenever the need arose.

The human population has multiplied exponentially in the past three thousand to four thousand years. Currently there are more than seven billion people living on earth. These people's demand for new products continues to grow by leaps and bounds. Innovative products are made possible by the advancements of science and technology. Consumers' desire for things to enjoy is at an all-time high. A great deal of land has been cleared for the purpose of developing it. A great deal of food needs to be produced to feed all the people who exist. New mines and oilfields have been explored. Since the resources on earth are scarce, knowledge in areas such as finance, economics, banking, and so forth has been developed to assess the viability of projects and to predict the outcome from the utilization of scarce resources. Indirectly all these financial decisions eventually shape the economic activities undertaken in every nook and cranny of the globe.

The ongoing scientific research, especially in the field of engineering, leads to the creation of more complex forms of mathematical expression to enhance accuracy in accounting and to predict the functionality of dams, aircraft, automobiles, and so forth, as well as the soundness, safety, and efficiency of those products.

A computer chip manipulates a myriad of sequences from electrically signalled input and then transforms that information into a corresponding outcome of electric signals, which are displayed on a monitor as a meaningful message to the user. It is amazing to see computer chips nowadays operate at gigahertz. The prefix *giga-* implies that sequences of binary "instructions" numbering in the thousands of millions are manipulated every second by the chip. In short, the primary function of a computer chip is to make binary computations. Generally, people assume that the answer to a mathematical computation arrived at by a computer has to be correct, but we should take note that the circuitry of a computer chip has its limitations and flaws. We should be aware of the computer's limits, and judge its accuracy with an open mind.

People nowadays seem to simply accept the validity of the majority of complex mathematical expressions as they have been taught to understand them without questioning their accuracy and logic. This indicates that there is a pitfall to rote learning. The major objective of this book is to shed some new light on the essential field of mathematics by highlighting some possible errors that most common people do not realize exist. These errors have been in effect for centuries, or in some cases for thousands of years – since the concept of mathematics was formulated. This book will remind us of the need to perform constant research and to re-examine the knowledge that we have gained in school or at university. Doing so will at least enhance our understanding of the knowledge we have received. Besides, the knowledge that we have in the fields of mathematics and science is useful to us only after we ascertain its validity. Only accurate knowledge will pave the way for advancement in the future of humankind. On the contrary, erroneous knowledge will hinder our understanding of natural phenomena and, at the same time, make learning become a pain, as happened with quantum physics. Any wise person should be able to master the technique of gauging knowledge as correct or incorrect without any difficulties. If a particular theory is claimed to be superior to others but only a handful of people can comprehend it entirely, then it is not an insult to the person who proposed the theory to say that it is truly useless. In other words, any accurate theory should be able to be grasped by any individual whose intelligence is above average. It is ironic to me that those who once claimed to understand quantum theories may actually not understand them at all, because quantum theories seem to have lost touch with reality. Quantum theories have constantly clashed with reality, as they fail to explain even the simplest natural phenomenon, like why nuclear energy has been classified as a non-renewable source of energy in light of Albert Einstein's famous equation $E = mc^2$. Just because a theory is established does not mean that it should be regarded as 100 per cent correct! The biggest problem we face, though, is that erroneous knowledge could possibly bring darkness, hindering humankind from advancing. In conclusion, only a correct knowledge of mathematics and the sciences will ensure continuous prosperity for humankind. And to ensure future prosperity, humankind needs to constantly re-examine and research pre-existing knowledge. We also need to develop new theories to provide us with a better understanding of pre-existing ones. The author stresses that humankind always needs to look back on the knowledge we have and ensure that it is correct and proper, as the knowledge we have is a stepping stone for our advancement in the future!

How the Numerical System, Arithmetic, and Complex Mathematical Concepts Are Related

The basic purpose of numbers is that they are used for counting. Normally, children are taught to count as if counting involves numbers only. The unit is left out. In reality, counting with numbers only is meaningless. When we count, we leave out the unit because we have been taught to count that way. But unconsciously we know what we are counting every time we are counting. If we count the number of apples that are in a basket, then we ignore the oranges and pears that are in the same basket. Provided that we want to count the number of fruits in a basket, we consider them all – apples, oranges, and pears – as if they are the same. This is because apples, oranges, and pears are all fruits. Basically, when we are counting, the unit is always applied, but we always choose to ignore it. In conclusion, true counting must include both the number and its corresponding unit.

Normally, the whole numbers, such as zero, one, two, three, four, and so forth, are used to quantify objects in their natural state of existence, like apples in a basket. When we count apples, every single apple can be regarded as a unit of apple. On the other hand, every apple is definitely different from the rest of apples in the same basket in terms of weight, colour, shape, and size. But we just presume that all the apples in the same basket are exactly identical to one another. This is the basic assumption we make when we are counting the number of apples in the basket.

In ancient times, before the invention of integers, words such as *gain*, *surplus, savings, debt, loan, shortage,* and *deficit* (in whatever language) were used to denote their mathematical equivalences. In modern times, *gain, surplus,* and *savings* are words associated with positive integers. Normally a positive integer can also be written as a number with or without a positive sign before it. For instance, a surplus of five apples can be expressed as "five apples" or "+5 apples". Basically, a positive integer denotes something that is real and tangible, now or in the near future.

On the other hand, the word *deficit* has been used to denote a negative integer. Nowadays a minus sign before a number is used to denote a negative integer. For instance, "negative five apples" or "-5 apples" is used to denote something that is virtual and normally imaginary, like something that has already been consumed or something that you have borrowed from somebody and are required to return to that person. This implies that a negative integer is a description of something that is normally intangible. For example, even if you have a particular amount of money with you now, you will soon part with it because you have to repay it to someone in near future. In short, the money seems like it does not belong to you; thus, the money seems intangible, even though, of course, the money is not at all intangible in real time. While zero is neither imaginary nor real, it just implies emptiness, like a vacuum – that's all. Therefore, zero should not be accompanied by any unit at all.

We often confuse the positive sign of a positive integer with the plus sign of addition. The same is true of the negative; we confuse the negative sign of a negative integer with the minus sign of subtraction. Therefore, we must differentiate between the negative or positive sign of an integer number and the subtraction or addition symbol. It is paramount to place brackets where necessary to avoid ambiguity.

Is the subtraction of negative five apples a mathematically sound prospect? Some of us would be quick to confirm that the subtraction of negative five apples is equivalent to plus five apples. As is the case with the negative sign of subtraction, when a negative integer is multiplied with negative five apples, the product is a positive number. Before we answer the question posed at the beginning of this paragraph, we have to understand the meaning of negative or positive integers and define the meaning of the arithmetic operations of addition or subtraction. When it is said that there are negative five apples, this implies that there are either five imaginary apples or five apples that a person can't consume because he or she is required to return them to a creditor later on (i.e. the individual has consumed the apples that he or she borrowed much earlier, and those apples he or she now possesses cannot be consumed because they need to be returned to the creditor). This may imply that the original five apples have already been consumed and are no longer in existence. Therefore, it is impossible for a person to consume those apples, because they are intangible. Also, one should not consume something that he or she has promised to pay back. In a nutshell, a person cannot consume something that is intangible, like negative five apples, and should not consume something that he or she owes to someone else. In conclusion, the subtraction of negative five apples is not logical at all. We are sure that the answer is definitely *not* positive five apples since it is not operable – because its operation is illogical.

The word *from* often follows the word *subtract*. Therefore, we usually say "subtracted from". For instance, "subtract five apples from eight apples" implies that we should take away five real apples from those eight apples, leaving three apples behind. In another example, subtracting negative eight apples from five apples is not logical at all, because all those five apples are real and there aren't any imaginary apples besides those five apples to subtract from. Logically, subtracting negative eight apples from five apples will not equate to thirteen real apples. Only adding five real apples to another eight apples would make the sum be thirteen apples. This very example implies that it does not take two negatives to make a positive. Again we should distinguish the negative sign of subtraction from the negative sign that signifies an imaginary object.

Our numerical system lays out the fundamentals of numbering. A number itself has little meaning unless it has been defined properly according to a particular set of definitions within a numerical system. Since human beings have eight fingers plus two thumbs, whenever we are counting we use a numerical system based on ten. First things first, though: we should correctly define the numerical system based on ten before we formulate more-complex mathematical concepts. The most basic of the complex mathematical concepts is simple arithmetical manipulation – the use of addition, subtraction, multiplication, and division. Furthermore, the validity of more-complex mathematical concepts (i.e. complicated mathematical equations) can be tested by inputting one or two variables with the value of one plus the respective unit. The rest of the variables are assumed to be zero for purposes of simplification. If a complicated mathematical equation that has been simplified still fails to get a logical answer that is plausibly correct vis-à-vis a natural phenomenon, then that complex equation would definitely be unreliable for use when trying to account for the complex phenomenon. In other words, if the outcome of a simplified mathematical equation is not correct or logical when it comes to describing a natural phenomenon, then it has no usefulness as a complex mathematical equation. Any mathematical operation must be logical and sensible when describing a natural phenomenon.

Multiplication

Obviously, many people would strongly agree that the values of both the square of positive two $(+2)^2$ and negative two $(-2)^2$ would equate to positive four, or four (4). A negative number such as negative two (-2) signifies something that is intangible or imaginary, and might be used to describe something that has already been consumed.

Referring to Figure 1 and Figure 2, clearly there are four squares in each of the two diagrams. But there are four imaginary boxes in Figure 1, where dotted lines have been used to denote something that is virtual, which means that it is intangible. There are four real boxes in Figure 2 that have been marked with solid lines. In reality, an imaginary number multiplied by another imaginary number will not produce a real object. Therefore, it is wrong to assume that a negative number multiplied by another negative number will produce a product with a positive number, as there are four imaginary boxes in Figure 1 as opposed to four real boxes in Figure 2.

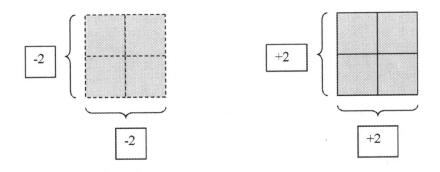

Without any ambiguity, a negative integer signifies something that is imaginary (i.e. negative magnitude denotes an imaginary object, for instance something that has been consumed), which means that it is intangible. On the other hand, positive-integer numbers denote something that is real, which is usually tangible.

It is naïve to believe that one imaginary number multiplied by another imaginary number will result in a product indicating a real object. The previous example makes the distinction between four imaginary boxes and four real boxes. Generally it is not valid to believe that multiplying a negative dimension of a square with another of its negative dimensions in an attempt to quantify the number of boxes that are contained within the square will provide one with the total number of real boxes within the square. Obviously, something imaginary only exists in our imagination, or our mental space. So the product of multiplying two imaginary numbers does not equal a real object. In a nutshell, any mathematical concepts must comply with the law of conservation of matter and the law of conservation of energy, since the total amount of matter and energy within the entire universe is a constant (i.e. the total mass of matter and the sum of all various forms of energy within the universe are constants). Something real cannot suddenly become imaginary. This is in parallel with the belief that matter can be neither created nor destroyed. Similarly, the total of all the various forms of energy within the universe is also a constant. But the magnitude of each denomination of various energy types or matter within the universe may be different from time to time, keeping in line with different dynamic states brought about by the expansion of the universe.

In reality, the process of multiplication is derived from the operation of addition. Obviously, one needs to memorize the contents of the multiplication table before one can masterfully solve multiplication problems. Take for instance five rows of boxes, with each row having two boxes. What is the total number of boxes in the five rows of boxes? The answer is ten boxes, because five times two equals ten, based on the multiplication table. If we find the sum of five twos, then we get the same answer. It is very important to understand that multiplication is directly derived from addition. The product of a multiplication problem can be checked for accuracy by comparing it to its equivalent addition problem's sum. If the product found by multiplying is not the same as the sum derived from the multiplication problem's equivalent addition problem, then the answer provided by the equivalent summation must be correct. In other words, the addition supersedes the multiplication. This indirectly implies that something in the logic of the multiplication process could be wrong. Otherwise, *both* answers that are derived from the equivalent summation and multiplication should be exactly the same.

Modern mathematicians believe that performing the negation process on a number actually leads the number to jump from one end of a coordinate to the opposite end of the coordinate. This is commonly recognized as the negation process. For instance, performing the negation process on negative two apples would lead to the outcome of positive two apples. Logically adding four apples to the "shortage" of two apples (i.e. the two eaten apples were those that had been borrowed with the promise of paying them back later) would equal two apples, which would be the simplest equivalent summation of this negation manipulation. When the person pays back two of the four apples he had borrowed earlier, he is left with two apples. This is the closest equivalent summation of a negation process on negative two apples.

On the other hand, according to the current definition of *negation*, the negation process performed on positive two apples leads one to discover that there is a shortage of two apples, or negative two apples. The equivalent addition process would assume that the person consumed four apples from the two apples. By the same token, he must have consumed four apples altogether. In such a case, the two apples that he originally had and the other two apples that he borrowed would be the closest equivalent "addition" manipulation to use when describing the negation process on positive two apples.

Two similar negation processes possess two distinctively different addition equivalences: receiving an additional four apples and consuming four apples. Since there are two distinctively different summation equivalences for the same negation process, these strongly suggest that the logic of the negation process may not be correct. The multiplication process is directly derived from summation manipulation. Therefore, for every multiplication process, there is an equivalent summation process. The multiplication process and the summation process should both have as a result the same operation. This applies to the negation process too (i.e. both negation processes should have the same summation, in which the process of negation and its equivalent, the process of summation, must provide the same explanation and be consistent. Otherwise, the negation process could be wrong, as it violates the sanctity of logic: its equivalent summation).

Most mathematicians would perceive multiplication and division as being more superior to addition and subtraction since multiplication and division must precede addition and subtraction in the order of operations. It is problematic that all arithmetic problems are set up without the inclusion of the respective units, as if only numbers were involved in the computations. If units are included in any arithmetic problem, then it is obvious why multiplication and division must precede addition and subtraction. Take for example the simple arithmetic problem 8 – 5 × 2 + 6 ÷ 3, which includes no unit that needs to be resolved. In the previous section, the author stressed that numbers cannot stand alone and, therefore, must accompany their corresponding units. Just assume that such a problem has something to do with apples. When we plug units into the equation, it looks like this: 8 apples – 5 apples / row × 2 rows + [(6 apples ÷ 3 rows) × 1 row].

The number 5 must accompany the unit of apples per row, and the unit for 2 must be rows, so that the numbers are multipliable where the row(s) will be struck out, leaving only apples. In other words, the unit for the product of the multiplication problem must be equal to apples, a unit similar to the preceding term, namely 8 apples. Undoubtedly the problem of 5 apples/row × 2 rows must be solved first before subtracting from the preceding term, 8 apples.

For the terms of 6÷3, the number 6 should have apples as its unit, similar to its preceding term, 8 apples. Therefore, 3 must accompany each unit row in order for 6 to be divided by 3. The outcome unit of this division problem would be apples/row. The unit apples/row must be made equal to the unit, apple(s). But the unit apples/row is multiplied by an extra term, 1 row, so that the row cancels out and the unit, apple(s), remains.

The final answer of the computation is not zero apples. This is because zero is emptiness, which is dimensionless. Therefore the correct outcome of the computation is simply zero, as shown below.

8 – 5 × 2 + 6 ÷ 3 = ?

→ 8 apples – 5 apples/row × 2 rows + [(6 apples ÷ 3 rows) × 1 row] =
→ 8 apples – 10 apples + 2 apples = 0 apples
→ 0 apples = 0

---

8 apples – 5 apples/row × 2 rows + 6 apples ÷ 3 rows × 1 row = ?

We left out brackets and parentheses from the equation shown above, but with the proper notation in place, the process of computation becomes clear as to which calculation(s) should be performed first and which should be carried out later. In conclusion, multiplication and division should be performed first, before addition and subtraction, in order to keep the unit of computation consistent (i.e. the outcome unit of computation of all terms must be consistent;

the example unit of the foregoing calculation is apples). At the same time, the addition and subtraction should be made multipliable (i.e. the apples of the first term and the apple/row of the second term can't add up together because the units are not consistent. Furthermore, apples/row multiplied by rows would be performed first before subtracting from eight apples, which is the first term. On the other hand, the row of the fifth term (three rows) can't be multiplied with the row of the sixth term (one row), which is an additional term, as doing so would complicate the units, making them row². Therefore, one should take the number of apples of the fourth term and divide that number by the row of the fifth term should before multiplying by the row of the sixth term so that the unit will transform into apples. In terms of superiority, the addition and subtraction should turn out to be superior to multiplication and division since multiplication and division are derived from addition and subtraction. In conclusion, because of the importance of streamlining the units that are involved in the arithmetical computation, multiplication and division should be performed first, before addition and subtraction. Because of this, multiplication and division have always been seen as being superior to addition and subtraction, which is a misconception.

The Finite World and the Way to Differentiate Rational Numbers from Irrational Numbers

We live in a finite world, one in which the total amount of energy and the total amount of matter within the universe will always remain as constants even if energy can transform from one form to another (i.e. more and more transverse and rotational kinetic energy and magnetic energy will gradually transform into universal gravitational potential energy in parallel to the expansion of the universe, where all celestial objects will experience slowdown as they move farther and farther away from the centre of the universe. Somehow the total amount of various energy will remain as a constant). Indirectly, this implies that everything within the universe must obey the law of the conservation of energy. The universe is also duly obeying the law of conservation of matter (i.e. the total amount of matter within the universe is a constant), which directly or indirectly implies that Albert Einstein's famous equation $E = mc^2$ is incorrect, as a minuscule amount of matter cannot actually transform into an enormous amount of energy. This is simply because all radioactive substances are non-renewable sources of energy. If $E = mc^2$ is correct, then any material could be used to manufacture an atomic bomb. One would not necessarily have to have a *heavy* radioactive substance, such as uranium or plutonium. Some might argue vehemently that the detonation of atomic bombs in Hiroshima and Nagasaki during World War II was a testament that Albert Einstein's famous equation $E = mc^2$ is correct! Later, the author will discuss the process of detonating an atomic bomb in order to illustrate that no matter, especially heat and other energy that is released during an atomic bomb's explosion, is actually transforming into anything during such an occurrence.

Energy cannot be transformed into matter, so the total amount of matter within the entire universe must be a constant. Undoubtedly, photons are particles and can easily permeate a system the way heat does. The mass of a photon is minuscule, so its impact may be negligible. Everything within a closed system of an experiment, including all variables involved and all outcomes of mathematical computations, must be expressed in rational numbers. In other words, the number of atoms and molecules within a closed system should remain the same before and after the experiment. But the number of photons may not be exactly the same before and after the experiment, as heat may seep into or out of the system. Since the heat gain or loss within a closed system is considered minute when compared to the heat that is released during a nuclear explosion, it is difficult to quantify the difference before and after the experiment in terms of photon gain or loss, or heat gain or loss. On the other hand, when we have an experiment performed within a closed system where there is an obvious difference in weight before and after the experiment, this difference must be due to the large number of dynamic photons that have crossed the boundary of the closed system, like with the process of radioactivity. The mass of a single photon is so minuscule that it is beyond our capability to quantify; thus, the mass of photons is always a negligible variable. Then again, this does not directly imply that photons are massless. Their masses are just too difficult to be quantified with accuracy and precision – that's all! On the other hand, a closed system that has lost a gargantuan number of stationary photons (the photons that stick onto nucleons are called stationary photons. They somehow still puzzle us. We wonder, *How are they able to transform back into dynamic photons?* They are like compressed springs when they are perched on nucleons. The localized magnetic field of the nucleon is believed to play an important role in dislodging those stationary photons and turning them back into dynamic photons, or else in encouraging dynamic photons to adhere to those nucleons. It is precisely the change in terms of intrinsic spinning rates, ambient temperature, the external magnetic field's strength, the nucleon's angular momentum strengths, the flexure of quarks within nucleons, and localized and universal gravitational energy that enables these changes in terms of exchanging photons' rates on those nucleons) would be perceived to have an obvious weight *loss*, which strongly proves that photons possess mass, especially during particular types of radioactivity processes within a significant period of time. The heat gain or loss during a chemical reaction is perceived to be significant, yet the number of dissipated or absorbed photons that have crossed the boundary normally do not show any sign of significant change in weight before and after the chemical reaction. Chemists have made the mistake of thinking that chemical energy is energy derived from electrons after the process of electron sharing has taken place among all reactants. Undoubtedly, electron sharing makes it possible for chemical reactions to take place. Let's not forget that the nucleus structure (protons do not sit close to one another within the unique nucleus structure, whereas neutrons try to diffuse the tension among protons, so nucleons of an element arrange themselves in a unique way, which is called a unique nucleus structure) of an element is different before and after a chemical reaction, which strongly suggests that dynamic photons must have been either absorbed by or emitted from the nucleus. Sometimes, a unique orbital may take the place of the unique nucleus structure of the reactant. In other instances, the unique nucleus structure moulds the shape, orientation, configuration, and size of the orbital. In short, the unique orbital and the unique nucleus structure affect each other. Since nucleons are much larger than electrons, nucleons have a larger storage space for stationary photons. Without any doubt, a large portion of the chemical energy must be derived from the nucleus rather than from the electrons alone.

If Einstein's atomic theory is correct, then nuclear scientists can use virtually anything to manufacture an atomic bomb as long as it consists of matter. Why are very dense radioactive substances such as uranium 235 used to make atomic bombs whereas plutonium is used for the more powerful hydrogen bombs? All radioactive substances are classified as non-renewable sources of energy. This strongly suggests that there is an enormous amount of excess energy locked within the nuclei of radioactive substances (i.e. nucleons of very dense radioactive substances are saturated with an excess amount of stationary photons; therefore, the strength of their angular momentum is extreme, even though it is barely able to defy the presence of tremendously strong repulsive electrostatic forces coming from the large number of protons) that is rather unstable. Therefore, these elements tend to restructure their nuclei (i.e. they decay). It is believed that all radioactive substances were created during the Big Bang, and that the expansion of the universe will continuously weaken the angular momentum of those nucleons, which is what paves the way for those radioactive substances to decay. In other words, the dense nuclear structure of these substances, where there are just too many protons squeezed within a nucleus, is one of the main reasons that most very dense elements are radioactive substances. As a result of the weakening angular momentum of their nucleons, the forced restructuring of their unstable nuclear structure is inevitable before a radioactive element's nuclei are reduced in size.

On the other hand, nowadays there are plenty of man-made light radioactive substances that are manufactured by exposing non-radioactive substances to radioactivity in a nuclear reactor. Absorbing the abundance of dynamic photons and capturing energetic neutron(s) indirectly energizes these man-made substances. The presence of energetic neutrons disrupts the stability of the unique nucleus structure, where nucleons try to balance themselves in terms of their angular-momentum-based strength, which likely triggers restructuring of the entire unique nucleus itself. The balance between the repulsive electrostatic forces among protons within a nucleus structure and the strength of the angular momentum of nucleons indirectly determines the half-life of a radioactive substance. A short half-life suggests that the angular momentum is too weak to resist the strength of repulsive electrostatic forces among the protons within the unique nucleus structure.

Generally, the nucleus structure of uranium 235 is quite stable since the half-life of uranium 235 is 7.04×10^8 years (assuming that the nuclear scientists are correct in gauging the half-life of uranium 235), which is a rather long duration. Only the absorption of moderated neutron(s) would hasten the process of decay for uranium 235 nuclei. (All emitted free neutrons from most very dense radioactive substances are energetic neutrons. On the other hand, moderated neutrons contain much fewer stationary photons; therefore, they have rather weak angular momentum. Fast energetic neutrons that have collided with an array of carbon molecules within the lattice of graphite are forced to shed a sizeable number of stationary photons before they are transformed into moderated neutrons through inelastic collision. To be more precise, energetic neutrons cause the carbon molecules in the lattice of graphite to slide while they are colliding with carbon's lattice; subsequently, those fast energetic neutrons transform into moderated neutrons that subsequently move slower. The presence of a moderated neutron or moderated neutrons after they have been captured within the nuclei of uranium 235 poses a threat to the nuclear structure's stability because these moderated neutrons are likely to "steal" stationary photons from other nucleons in the vicinity. This causes a disruption to the distribution of stationary photons among nucleons. Of course, the presence of a weaker moderated neutron would be unable to prop up the rest of nucleons that are resting on top of it. Subsequently, that portion of the unique nucleus structure would cave in, initiating a restructuring of the entire unique nucleus structure; thus, the absorption of moderated neutron(s) would definitely hasten the decay.) Experimental proof shows that uranium 235 that has absorbed fast energetic neutrons does not experience a hastening decay of its radioactivity. This indirectly implies that fast energetic neutrons are seemingly compatible with most of the nucleons of uranium 235.

Experimental data show that the half-life of uranium 236 (2.34×10^7 years) is slightly shorter than the half-life of uranium 235 (7.04×10^8 years). Obviously, uranium 236 is a man-made element. (It is very unlikely that uranium 236 is derived from thorium 232 absorbing an alpha particle; otherwise, there would be abundance of uranium 236 on earth, since there is an abundance of thorium 232.) The absorption of a single energetic neutron by uranium 235 might produce uranium 236. Emitted fast energetic neutrons would likely shed only some photons to the surrounding area, even without colliding with anything, before being absorbed by the nucleus of uranium 235. Since the existence of uranium 236 is rather rare, the possibility that uranium 235 will capture an energetic neutron is extremely slim. In conclusion, the compatibility of an absorbed energetic neutron or neutrons by other elements determines the durability of the respective element's half-life.

Actually nuclear energy is energy that is harnessed from those stationary photons that adhere to nucleons of radioactive substances before they are released into the surrounding area during the nuclear restructuring process, where a dense nucleus transforms to become several much smaller and simpler nuclei. Obviously smaller nuclei contain fewer protons, so the repulsion forces among protons will be rather weak when compared to the nuclei of much denser radioactive substances. Therefore, less strenuous angular moment of the nucleons suffice to maintain the stability of their simpler nucleus structure. Whatever substance the excess stationary photons use in order to stick to the nucleons of those denser radioactive substances would be released to the surrounding area during the fission process, which is the restructuring of a nucleus. To trigger a sustainable chain reaction, the presence of graphite is needed in order to transform energetic neutrons into moderated neutrons and hasten the decay of those uranium 235 atoms. The graphite captures those moderated neutrons to ensure that more energetic neutrons are released from decaying uranium 236 so as to further fuel the chain reaction on other uranium 235 atoms. When the colossal nuclei of uranium 235 atoms are decaying simultaneously, an atomic detonation takes place, wherein tremendous heat is dissipated outwardly from ground zero. Surmounting released heat causes the nucleons of uranium 235 to dance agitatedly to the extent that even the absorption of energetic neutrons will effectively trigger the restructuring of what used to be the stable unique nucleus structure of uranium 235. The ability to destabilize uranium 235's unique nucleus structure even by absorbing energetic neutrons hastens the rate of decay tremendously. The successful detonations of atomic bombs at Hiroshima and Nagasaki indirectly infer that there is a tremendous number of stationary photons trapped within individual nuclei of especially very dense radioactive substances like uranium and plutonium. This also strongly suggests that some uranium 235 atoms might emit numerous energetic neutrons, rather than three energetic neutrons, whenever they are decaying, as is commonly believed by most nuclear scientists. Otherwise, it is rather difficult to achieve a sustainable chain reaction within a short period of time (e.g. several seconds).

The detonation of an atomic bomb clearly proves that atomic energy is *never* derived from transforming a minuscule amount of matter into an enormous amount of heat.

During radioactive decay, excess energy is released into the surrounding area from the split nucleus when stationary photons transform into dynamic photons as they dissipate into the surroundings. This energy is commonly recognized as a gamma ray (if the intensity is extremely high) or else is considered to be released heat (if the intensity is lower). Restructuring of the mother element's nucleus structure is inevitable and leads to a weakening of the angular momentum of nucleons, as if nuclei have brains and know that smaller daughter nuclei require less strenuous angular momentum to maintain the stability of the new and much smaller nucleus structure. Therefore, the much larger mother nucleus reduces in size to become the much smaller daughter nuclei, which require less strenuous angular momentum to maintain their nucleus structure's stability. After all, excess energy within the nuclei of radioactive substances has now been released and no more radioactivity will emerge, as the element has eventually transformed into a non-radioactive substance. Undoubtedly, non-radioactive substances have a much more stable unique nucleus structure, one wherein the various energies (i.e. angular momentum, electrostatic forces, gravitational forces, and magnetic forces) that are trapped within the nucleus have been harmonized with one another. Some radioactive substances must undergo several cycles of radioactive decay before they eventually become non-radioactive substances, which have no more excess energy trapped within their nuclei. Also, and obviously, much fewer stationary photons adhere to the nucleons of the daughters' nuclei, and thus these are classified as non-radioactive substances. Obviously Einstein's $E = mc^2$ cannot be right in asserting that nuclear energy is harnessed by transforming a minuscule amount of matter into a tremendous volume of energy (i.e. the phrase *nuclear energy* usually refers to the amount of heat that is released by a radioactive substance when its nucleus decays. Precisely, heat is the number of dissipated photons per volume per time)!

In the 1980s, American scientists proved that photons are particles that register on an extremely sensitive electronic balance as having a weight when a light is shone on them. This is the most convincing proof that light is made up of particles called photons and that dynamic photons possess momentum. Only dynamic matter possesses momentum. Quantum physicists are wrong in believing that photons are massless. They believe this simply because a dynamic vacuum should not possess any momentum at all. If electromagnetic waves are massless particles, then there will be no impact on the electronic balance when the electromagnetic waves knock against it. Electromagnetic waves are nothing more than a finite number of dissipated photons per volume per time. Obviously, human beings' capabilities to determine such things are limited to a certain extent. For instance, the mass of a single photon is impossible to quantify with accuracy and precision by using any hi-tech electronic gadgets. Thus, we cannot provide proof that photons are massless, like a vacuum. Similarly, we may never know how many stationary photons are contained within a nucleus. Needless to say, we cannot know the exact number of stationary photons on an individual nucleon within a nucleus.

We have more reasons to believe that electromagnetic waves are dissipated photons per volume per time rather than elusive waves that consist of a magnetic field and an electric field that are perpendicular to one another. Place two matchsticks outside in the sun. Use a magnifying glass to focus sunlight on the head of one matchstick (make sure the head of a matchstick is at focal length from the magnifying glass), and place the other matchstick under direct sunlight. Without any doubt, the head of the matchstick that is under the magnifying glass will burst into flame. The magnifying glass is simply concentrating an abundance of dynamic photons into a small dot at its focal point. With the availability of an abundance of dynamic photons per volume per time on the head of a matchstick, the stationary electrons are more likely to absorb more photons per time than the ones that dissipate into the surroundings; therefore, those more massive electrons travel farther away from nuclei. Of course, the nuclei of molecules also absorb an abundance of photons. This leads the nucleus to wobble, and also causes the nuclear structure to flex as it gets ready for a chemical reaction to take place. Obviously, the enlarging orbital of various chemical compounds on the head of a matchstick overlapping each other initiates the chemical reaction (i.e. the chemical compounds on the head of a matchstick are a mixture of sulphur and potassium chlorate. Potassium chlorate supplies oxygen, which is needed to oxidize sulphur). This indirectly infers that the presence of intense heat can initiate a chemical reaction because the enlargement of the orbital allows the orbitals to overlap, and this allows the sharing of electrons to take place. Furthermore, the enlargement of the orbital also leads to a modification of the nucleus structure of a chemical compound to get it set for a subsequent chemical reaction, which also causes permanent modification of the nucleus structure. In other words, any modification on the orbital influences the unique nucleus structure and gets the element ready to initiate a chemical reaction, which leads to a permanent modification of the orbital once a new unique nucleus structure is set after the chemical reaction.

Obviously, sunlight focused on a point by using a magnifying glass is more powerful than direct sunlight, since the former can trigger a chemical reaction. It is naïve to believe that the frequency of sunlight will change after it has passed through a magnifying glass. Quantum scientists reckon that the higher frequencies of electromagnetic waves are more powerful than the lower frequencies. Quantum scientists presume that focused sunlight is more powerful than direct sunlight and believe, therefore, that focused sunlight must have a higher frequency. Experimental observation of passing waves in a ripple tank clearly shows that the frequency of waves before entering a lens and after passing out of the lens remains the same. In other words, the frequency of the waves within a lens is no different from the frequency before the waves enter the lens and pass out of the lens. This indirectly suggests that even if sunlight is an elusive wave, its frequency before entering a magnifying glass is exactly the same as the frequency right after it exits from the lens. Focused sunlight is more powerful than direct sunlight, but not because focused sunlight has a higher frequency.

This natural phenomenon can be better understood if we assume that all forms of electromagnetic waves are dissipated photons per volume per time, where the gamma ray has the highest number of dynamic photons per volume per time; therefore, the gamma ray is the most powerful form of electromagnetic wave. Gamma rays can pierce through very thick heavy metal, like a lead sheet. On the other hand, X-rays are able to penetrate only a thin metal sheet. Since a gamma ray has a colossal number of dynamic photons per volume per time, a significantly higher number than the X-ray has, a rather large number of dissipated photons eventually manage to exit from the other end of a thick metal sheet despite the fact that an abundance of dynamic photons are absorbed by the nuclei of that metal's atoms. This indirectly also implies that there are plenty of void nuclei, making it possible for the gamma ray to penetrate a thick lead plate. Stationary electrons also absorb some of the gamma ray's dynamic photons, but they are small in size and are always on the move, which enables them to experience only a limited rate of exchange of photons with the gamma ray. Dynamic photons possess momentum, and the higher number of dynamic particles (i.e. particles are matter that contain mass and fill up space) per volume per time have greater power. If those dynamic photons possess slightly higher velocities, they are perceived to have greater power than the slower-moving photons. Therefore, the number of dynamic photons per volume per time and their velocities determine the power of any electromagnetic wave. The author believes that not all dynamic photons possess the same velocity, a velocity that has been recognized as the speed of light. My observation of astronomical phenomena strongly suggests the existence of red shift and blue shift (red light is less powerful than blue light), which proves that the speed of light is not exactly a constant, as is widely believed by quantum scientists. Assuming that the intensity of light from the same star is approximately the same for a short duration, the changes in terms of kinetic energy directly affect the star's level of perceived energy, especially when the star is approaching the observer (i.e. blue shift) or moving farther and farther away from the observer (i.e. red shift). Obviously, dynamic photons that travel a much longer distance actually utilize additional energy in doing so. This slightly weakens their kinetic energy. Thus, observed light from a departing star appears to change its colour to red – what is commonly known as the red shift phenomenon. In contrast, the light from the approaching star changes its colour to bluish since the star's light has conserved more kinetic energy by travelling a shorter distance. Since the kinetic energy of dynamic photons is not a constant, photons with higher kinetic energy travel faster than those with lower kinetic energy, so the former are perceived as bluish-coloured stars rather than reddish ones. This strongly suggests that the speed of light (i.e. dissipated dynamic photons) is never a constant hinge on the level of the kinetic energy light possesses, which contradicts the belief widely accepted by quantum scientists that the speed of light is a constant.

In another convincing proof that light is made up of dissipated photons per volume per time rather than elusive waves is that the flame of a Bunsen burner changes from yellowish to bluish after the air aperture is opened. Obviously, bluish flame is hotter than yellowish flame. More air is allowed to mix with methane gas when the air aperture of the burner is opened fully. When the aperture is opened all the way, the methane gas burns more efficiently because more oxygen molecules are present. In other words, more methane molecules per volume per time are combusted than when the air aperture of the Bunsen burner is closed, which accounts for the fact that the bluish flame is hotter than the yellowish flame. When we place an asbestos board slightly above the yellowish flame, dark marks of carbon debris smear across it. Obviously, yellowish flame is also more "dirty"; it contains more carbon debris because it burns less efficiently. On the other hand, bluish flame leaves slight dark marks on the asbestos board. Undoubtedly, the bluish flame is cleaner and hotter. Similarly, the flame changes colour, from yellowish to bluish, because there is a higher number of dissipated photons per volume per time when more methane molecules per volume per time are burnt. The reason that the flame of a Bunsen burner changes from yellowish to bluish is not because the flame has changed its frequency. In a nutshell, the intensity of dissipated photons per volume per time determines the colour of the flame, and this has nothing to do with a change of frequency. It is naïve to assume that electromagnetic waves have dualistic characteristics, sometimes behaving like particles and other times behaving like elusive waves. The flame of a Bunsen burner is hot enough to boil water in a beaker. Boiled water swirls agitatedly within a hot beaker. Water molecules that absorb more dissipated photons from the flame than they dissipate into the atmosphere cause boiled water molecules to experience a sufficient change in momentum, which enables them to swirl vigorously inside the beaker. This clearly proves that heat consists of dissipated photons and that dynamic particles possess momentum. In other words, changes in terms of the stockpile of stationary photons in a molecule lead to changes in momentum. If we just accept the fact that light, heat, and all so-called electromagnetic waves are nothing more than dissipated photons per volume per time, we will understand readily that virtually all natural phenomena are related to electromagnetic waves.

The expanding universe will reach its maximum size one day in the future when the universal gravitational potential energy for all celestial objects that are near or at the brink of the universe reach their maximum displacement. After the universe has reached its maximum size, it will stop expanding. This will happen when all kinetic energy has been converted to universal gravitational potential energy. At this stage, the universe will stand still momentarily before starting to implode on account of the mutual attraction force among celestial objects. The speeds of these celestial objects will increase gradually as more and more of their universal gravitational potential energy is transformed back into kinetic energy as they head towards the centre of the universe. All celestial objects will possess maximum kinetic energy when they collide head-on near the centre of the universe. When this collision occurs, a big explosion will take place, because the celestial bodies will then have an extremely large amount of kinetic energy. Matter will be flung out from the centre of the universe upon impact. Again, all celestial objects will start to move outwards towards the edge of the universe. Their speed will decrease gradually as they move farther and farther away from the centre of the universe after the big explosion. More and more of their kinetic energy will be gradually converted into universal gravitational potential energy as they move farther and farther away from the centre of the universe.

Astronomical observation shows that the expansion of the universe is slowing down mainly because more and more kinetic energy is transforming back into universal gravitational potential energy as the size of the universe becomes larger and larger. As the universe gets bigger, celestial objects are more sparsely set apart from one another; thus, the gravitational pull among them is rather weak. If such were not the case, then more and more kinetic energy would transform into the universal gravitational potential energy and the rate of the universe's expansion would be accelerating rather than slowing down. The theory of the existence of dark matter might not be able to account for the slowing down of the expansion of the universe. If dark matter exists at all, it should constantly exist in every different dynamic state of the universe.

In other words, dark matter cannot just pop up suddenly in this phase of the expansion of the universe. The theory of the presence of dark matter does not help explain why the expansion rate of the universe is slowing down. As the universe is "ageing", astronomers realize that there are more black holes within the universe than ever before. Black holes suck in more and more matter from their vicinity. Even if the strength of mutually attracting universal gravitational forces among celestial bodies is weakening, the universe is enlarging in volume. Those dense black holes enable celestial objects to remain mutually attracted to one another even when they are thinly dispersed within an enlarging universe.

The foundation of mathematics is built upon logic and assumes that everything within the entire universe is finite (i.e. the total matter within the universe will always be a constant regardless of the universe's dynamic phase of expansion or contraction, since Einstein's $E = mc^2$ is not true). The exchange of photons among different forms of matter is a continuous process. It is impossible to precisely quantify the net gain or net loss of dynamic photons in a system since the mass of a single photon is beyond our capability to quantify. Also, we do not know exactly how many photons per time have been absorbed into or dissipated by a system. Somehow all scientific concepts must comply with the law of the conservation of energy and the law of the conservation of matter (i.e. the total amount of various energies is a constant even though various denominations of different forms of energy are subject to changes since one form of energy is allowed to transform into other form of energy/energies in keeping with the dynamic state of the universe. Similarly, the total amount of matter within the universe is a constant), in contrast to the conservation of energy-matter. This is because the conservation of energy-matter assumes that energy and matter are interchangeable, for example, a minuscule amount of matter is unable to transform into an enormous amount heat, like with the detonation of an atomic bomb, or vice versa. In addition, quantum scientists believe that gamma rays produce a pairing of an electron and a positron, assuming that photons are massless particles (all these beliefs have turned out to be untrue); thus, the total of energy and matter would be some finite "constants". Otherwise, we have no idea what the equilibrium point between matter and energy is. For instance, will all matter transform into energy, or will matter, up to a certain level, cease to transform into energy? Somehow, the total of energy-matter remains as a constant. Thank God that this last point is not true; otherwise, the dynamic state of energy and matter would be hard to predict. It would be difficult to determine whether all matter will eventually transform into energy or vice versa, or if it will end up being fifty-fifty, where matter and energy reach a state of equilibrium.

Einstein was definitely wrong to assume that the speed of light, c, is a constant. Imagine that dynamic photons are like athletes. They would be exhausted and tired after engaging in a great deal of physical activity. On the other hand, they would still be fresh and energetic after a hundred-metre race. Naturally, more energy is needed to do the additional work to complete a marathon than to participate in a hundred-metre race. Therefore, it depends on how much kinetic energy has been utilized to do work, how much kinetic energy has been transformed into other forms of energy, and how much kinetic energy is left. If a lot of a photon's kinetic energy is spent on doing work by transforming into other forms of energy, then the photon is left with less kinetic energy than it had initially. Without any doubt, photons with a lower concentration of kinetic energy travel at a slower velocity, because the level of kinetic energy is a yardstick of their velocity. For instance, if an athlete's initial position is on a hilltop, he will accelerate effortlessly when he is running towards the foothill. In contrast, if he races up to a hilltop, it will be more difficult for him to maintain his speed. The actual speed of light might vary depending on its initial position and also on where it is heading, whether it is moving towards the centre of the universe or heading towards the brink of the universe. In a nutshell, the speed of a photon depends on the level of kinetic energy it possesses. In reality, the speed of photons is definitely not a constant. Their speed depends solely on their level of kinetic energy. Their speed is higher when the amount of kinetic energy they hold is higher (here, the author is assuming that the content of the matter of every photon is invariable). Of course, the direction in which a photon is heading is also important when trying to gauge its speed. For instance, a photon that is travelling towards the centre of the universe will gradually accelerate as a result of transforming more and more of its universal gravitational potential energy into kinetic energy. On the other hand, any photons that are heading towards the edge of the universe will experience slowdown as more and more of their kinetic energy converts to universal gravitational potential energy. The speed of light, wherever light exists in the universe, is never a constant, which is contrary to the commonly held belief of most quantum scientists, including Einstein himself. Generally, all dynamic photons that we receive from the sun should be considered compatible in terms of the content of kinetic energy (assuming that both the sun and the earth are made of a similar material that originated from a similar location within the universe). On the other hand, some other dynamic photons from different locations within the universe, like those of distant stars, likely possess different levels of kinetic energy, as they must have done some work already before reaching the earth – and also depending on where they originate from. Since the mass of a single photon is minuscule, the differences between protons in terms of their kinetic energy are not significant regardless of where in the universe they originated.

The author strongly believes that the total number of photons and nucleons within the universe is finite even though it is impossible to quantify the exact number of photons that are trapped within nuclei and, needless to say, the exact number of photons on nucleons. Therefore, most natural phenomena must produce finite outcomes. For instance, a closed tin that contains boiling water seems to have the same weight after it has cooled off. Even though an abundance of dynamic photons dissipate through the sealed tin and into the surrounding area as the tin cools off gradually, the loss of photons is not significant enough to be detected, not even with the aid of a sensitive electronic balance. On the other hand, the radioactive-decay process is likely to show a significant loss of mass as a result of the tremendous number of dynamic photons that have been released into the surrounding area (i.e. dissipated), where changes in terms of mass and content are rather obvious. This indirectly implies that photons are particles and that therefore they possess mass. Then again, this does not infer that a minuscule amount of matter has been transformed into heat energy when a radioisotope has undergone the radioactive process. Most mathematical modelling of scientific phenomena we are dealing with should be finite, as the minuscule net gain or net loss of photons is negligible. Most irrational numbers make no logical sense at when used in parallel with the law of conservation of energy and the law of conservation of matter, with the exception of π (pi). Even though pi is an irrational number, this does not mean that the area of a circle is not finite. For a more detailed explanation of why the author believes π to be an irrational number, especially when used in the computation of the area of a circle, please refer to last topic in Chapter 1, "In Search of Pi (π)".

All input variables and outcomes involved in mathematical computations must be rational numbers. For instance, a lump of iron powder in a beaker is perceived as having no change in weight when it is placed in different environment, such as out in the sunlight or in a dark room. The number of iron atoms inside a beaker is fixed, and yet the iron atoms still constantly exchange photons at different rates in different surroundings. It is extremely difficult to know with certainty if those iron atoms are actually gaining photos from the environment or losing photons to the environment. There are only minuscule differences in the number of photons are involved; there is no obvious difference in terms of the iron atoms' perceived weight in a different environment. It is common practice to presume that the weight of iron atoms in a beaker will remain the same most of the time even at different locations. With this example, the author is trying to show that no system is *perfectly closed* where photons are concerned, mainly because photons are able to freely dissipate inside or outside the boundary of a closed system.

Generally, if input variables or outcomes of a computation (regarding a phenomenon) turn out to be irrational numbers, this cannot be correct because it has indirectly violated both the law of conservation of matter and the law of conservation of energy. With the detonation of an atomic bomb, where there is an obvious loss of mass afterwards, it has always been mistaken that a minuscule amount of matter has been transformed into an enormous amount of energy. This is because heat energy actually consists of dissipated photons, which indirectly implies that heat also possesses mass. A gargantuan amount of dynamic photons fling out from the split nuclei of uranium 235 (which is very dense), which accounts for the lost mass, despite some other emitted particles, such as the nuclei of helium, which are sometimes released into the surrounding area. Of course, it is rather impossible to quantify the mass of dissipated heat. Any matter that is exposed to heat will, somehow, experience a change in momentum, which clearly implies that heat consists of dissipated photons per volume per time. Undoubtedly, all natural phenomena are zero-sum phenomena, where something that is gained must have taken substance from something else. Some quantum scientists presume that electromagnetic waves like gamma rays are able to produce an electron and positron, as if matter can be derived from emptiness, since they believe that electromagnetic waves are like a vacuum, which is massless. In other words, quantum scientists believe that the universe was created out of nothing. Therefore, they conclude that something like an electron and positron pairing could be actually produced from nothing, like electromagnetic waves. Why, then, do gamma rays in a vacuum fail to produce an electron and positron pairing? The creation of an electron and a positron would likely have to take place when the gamma ray is targeted at a steel plate – and only once in a blue moon. New experimental proof shows that a gamma ray has a high number of dissipating photons per volume per time, which convincingly proves that a positron must be "triggered" from an iron atom and that such a positron would likely knock out an electron on its way out of the steel plate. The mechanism behind the triggering of a positron from an iron atom by way of the gamma ray is still not completely understood. In any event, the created positron by way of gamma ray is not necessarily accompanied by an electron every time. Indirectly this explains why gamma rays fail to produce the pairing of an electron and a positron in a vacuum. These new discoveries strongly suggest that the quantum scientists are wrong in thinking that the entire universe was created out of virtually nothing in a vacuum. There is no doubt that we can hardly quantify the content of matter down to the difference in the number of photons, but somehow we know that the total matter within the universe is a constant. Therefore, mathematical concepts and theories must deal with mostly rational figures in order to remain relevant and logical.

There are two very important irrational numbers, namely π and $\sqrt{2}$. Of course, these numbers have an infinite number of decimal places, but not all numbers with an infinite number of decimal places are irrational numbers. The fraction ⅓ has an infinite number decimal places too, 0.33333 ..., but it is a rational number. How do we distinguish between irrational numbers and rational ones? We can test to see if a number is rational or irrational by multiplying a whole number and the number in question. If the product is another whole number, then the tested number is a rational number. On the other hand, if there is no existence of a suggested whole number, where the product of multiplication is also another whole number, then the tested number is an irrational number.

whole number × rational number = whole number

A whole number must be something that can exist in the real world, like fifteen apples.

As stated above, ⅓ (i.e. 0.333333 ...) is a rational number even though it has an infinite number of decimal places. Just assume that there is a whole number, such as fifteen apples, and then multiply it by ⅓. The product is five apples, and 5 is a whole number. Therefore, the number ⅓ must be a rational number. It is similar for the number $^3/_{11}$. When eleven apples are multiplied by $^3/_{11}$, the product is three apples, even though $^3/_{11}$ (i.e. 0.272727 ...) has an infinite number of decimal places. One would be quick to point out that $\sqrt{2}$ could be a rational number too by allowing $\sqrt{2}$ apples to be multiplied with

$\sqrt{2}$, where the product is equal to two apples. The crucial problem is how to "make" $\sqrt{2}$ apples. As long as it is impossible to "find" a whole number to multiply with a tested number so that its product is another whole number, the tested number is recognized as an irrational number. The whole number must be something that is feasible in the real world, like fifteen apples or eleven apples, but definitely not $\sqrt{2}$ apples.

When the tested number is an irrational number, it is impossible to seek a whole number to multiply with the tested number so that the product is another whole number. Since irrational numbers possess an infinite number of decimal places, such as $\sqrt{2}$, which equals 1.41421356 ..., it is impossible for us to cut the apples to make one portion equal exactly $\sqrt{2}$ apples. After we cut an apple to the size of 41.4 per cent and add another apple, this does not exactly equal $\sqrt{2}$ apples. Cutting that apple to 41.42 per cent would be more accurate. Then again, 41.421 per cent would be even slightly more accurate. The attempt to seek a more accurate representation of $\sqrt{2}$ apples could go on forever simply because $\sqrt{2}$ has an infinite number of decimal places. It is impossible to take $\sqrt{2}$ apples and multiply them with $\sqrt{2}$ to obtain two apples. That the attempt to seek a whole number to multiply with a tested number so that the product is another whole number has failed directly implies that the tested number is indeed an irrational number. Both irrational and rational numbers can possess an infinite number of decimal places. The only difference is that a rational number can be multiplied by a whole number to produce another whole number. For example, multiplying ⅓ by 15 apples would equal 5 apples, where both 15 and 5 are whole numbers. In addition, we live in a finite world, as the amount of matter and energy within the entire universe is fixed. In contrast, irrational numbers most likely violate the law of conservation of matter and the law of conservation of energy. Since the law of conservation of matter and the law of conservation of energy are both correct, there is no room for most irrational numbers, the exception being π. The logic is that rational numbers make sense, whereas the majority of irrational numbers are unthinkable. In a nutshell, mathematics should only deal with rational numbers because they make sense and are logical (with the exception of π). Unlike rational numbers, the majority of irrational numbers are absurd, illogical, and senseless, defying the law of conservation of matter and the law of conservation of energy, with which most natural phenomena comply.

Absolute Numbers

The definition of an absolute number is as follows. For any number a:

$$|a| = \begin{cases} .a \text{ if } a \geq 0 \\ .-a \text{ if } a < 0 \end{cases}$$

It is not logical to believe that an object that is real and an object that is imaginary are the same when looked at through the lens of an "absolute" process. By the same token, the absolute value of $-a$ equates to $+a$. "Precisely real" and "virtual" contrast with one another. Furthermore, there isn't any process that could make them equate to one another. A good analogy for an application of absolute process is an image in a mirror, which is virtual and looks almost exactly like the object. The reflection of the object has the exact same size and features of the object itself. It is also the same distance away from the objects (or people) surrounding it. The only difference is that with the mirror image, the right side of the original object appears on the left side and the left side appears on the right. This indirectly illuminates the fact that the object and its mirror image are not exactly the same as each other. Obviously, the most important difference between an object and its corresponding mirror image is that the object is real whereas the mirror image is virtual.

Undoubtedly, absolute process has other applications, such as illustrating the oscillating flow of alternating current electricity. For an alternating current, the free electrons literally change the direction of their flow from time to time (the frequency of alternating current in most countries is 60 Hz, which implies that the current changes its direction of flow 120 times per second). Absolute process has commonly been used to indicate that the flow of the alternating current is fluctuating within a range of magnitude, namely $-a$ ampere and a ampere. In reality, every free electron that has been produced with a similar potential difference is almost identical to all the others in terms of the number of its stationary photons. This indirectly implies that not all free electrons under the same voltage are exactly identical to one another in terms of their number of stationary photons. But in reality, no two free electrons have the exact same number of stationary photons adhering to them. The general direction of flow of an alternating current per time indicates only the movement of the majority of the free electrons per time. It is wrong to believe that all free electrons in the circuit will flow in a particular direction before the flow is reversed and that this process repeats itself again and again endlessly. In reality, there is indeed a reasonable number of other types of free electrons that are flowing in the opposite direction, against the mainstream flow of the majority of free electrons (i.e. the mainstream flow has many more free electrons than it has other electrons flowing against those free electrons), at any one time, which ammeters fail to detect. The pointer of an ammeter oscillates between a positive and a negative reading every time the alternating current's free electrons shift the direction of their flow, as all free electrons travel in one particular direction in the electric circuit at any one time.

Every time an electromagnet in a transformer changes its magnetic polarity, there is a surging of current in the wire, which is the result of the change in the direction of the flow. It is a push-pull effect of the transformer that makes it possible to supply alternating current to cater to our power usage, as shown in Figure 3. Therefore, it is imperative that an electromagnetic be wrapped with dense solenoids so that during the push phase the magnetic field of the electromagnet will manage draw out the maximum number of free electrons from the transformer. Within the solenoid's copper atoms, there is deficit of electrons where some of the stationary electrons have been converted to free electrons under the induced magnetic field of the electromagnet, so those copper atoms "steal" electrons from the adjacent atoms along the cable that connects to the other end of the transformer and travels all the way to households as a result of the domino effect.

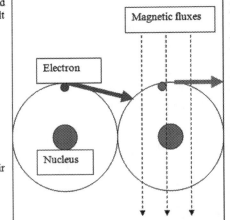

Pull-phase would induce as a result of the presence of unbalanced electrostatic force within adjacent atoms. Stationary electrons would be sucked into adjacent atoms as shown with blue arrow to "neutralize" their unbalanced electrostatic forces.

Magnetic fluxes

Electron

Nucleus

Push-phase takes place when the presence of a "strong" external magnetic field would "compact" magnetic field of stationary electrons to form an elastic magnetic field that enable them to attract more stationary photon from vicinity; subsequently, stationary electrons transform to free electrons before drifting towards adjacent atoms as indicated by a red arrow.

The push phase and the pull phase take place simultaneously and alternatively in the secondary solenoids within a transformer as a result of the alternating current in the primary solenoids, in which the electromagnet is constantly changing its magnetic polarity in parallel with the flow of alternating current in the primary circuit. The push phase must precede the pull phase and not vice versa. In addition, the free electrons of the push phase are much stronger than the ones that are created during the pull phase, mainly because push-phase free electrons are laden with an abundance of stationary photons (more so than pull-phase free electrons are).

During the push phase, stationary electrons constantly revolve around their nuclei because of the presence of strong external magnetic flux. The magnetic flux on these electrons interacts with external magnetic fluxes, where compact elastic magnetic flux forms around the electrons. The presence of more compact elastic magnetic flux allows those electrons to amass more dynamic photons from the surrounding area before transforming them into stationary photons. Subsequently, those stationary electrons transform into free electrons once they have gained sufficient mass and momentum to allow them to drift towards adjacent atoms as free electrons. The drifting direction of those free electrons is dictated by the orientation and configuration of the external magnetic flux of the electromagnet in a transformer, as shown on the right-hand side of Figure 3.

The pull phase takes place when adjacent atoms have lost a certain number of stationary electrons (i.e. the electrons that are confined within an atom). After they all have transformed into free electrons, they – especially those copper atoms of the secondary solenoid inside a transformer – are subject to unbalanced electrostatic forces within them, which drag stationary electrons from the adjacent atoms so as to defuse the extremely unbalanced electrostatic tension within them, as shown on the left-hand side of Figure 3. Push-pull effects manage to occur purely because the absolute strength of electrostatic charges on an electron is much weaker than that of a proton. If both an electron and a proton possess electrostatic charges of equal absolute strengths, even stationary electrons within the conductor's atoms will encounter difficulty when transforming into free electrons because protons within nuclei exert a strong pull on those electrons, which prevents them from transforming into free electrons.

Push-phase free electrons possess a huge amount of momentum; therefore, they can travel very long distances. This is because they are laden with an abundance of stationary photons. On the other hand, pull-phase free electrons lack momentum. They cannot travel far simply because they are not saturated with an abundance of stationary photons. We call these electrons "drifting electrons". One can only hope that they will saturate the secondary solenoids to get them ready for the next round of the push phase. Pull-induced electrons are not free electrons, as they are created in an attempt to defuse the unbalanced electrostatic charges within the copper atoms in the secondary solenoid.

Free electrons that flow in a particular direction along a wire will continue to do so until they have lost their momentum, at which point they will behave like the stationary electrons of the copper atoms along an electrical wire. Imagine a push-pull effect on a transformer that takes place at a very high frequency. This factor would indirectly be governed by the frequency of the turbines that drive the generator, where too high frequencies result in the dissipation of excess heat from the cable. On the other hand, too low of a frequency in the turbines results in the formation of weak induced magnetic fields by an electromagnetic in the transformer, which might not be optimal for producing a sufficient number of free electrons. The existing design and parameters of transformers, gas turbines, and generators cater to a current of 60 Hz in order to maximize the production of oscillating alternating current.

The reading on any ammeter is never accurate in gauging the exact number of free electrons that flow through a particular point of a circuit at any one time. This is because an ammeter is only able to measure the push-phase flow of free electrons and not the pull-phase flow of drifting electrons. An ammeter is only equipped to measure the one-way flow of the free electrons (which are in the majority) in a circuit at any one time simply because the fluctuation of the ammeter's pointer responds to the magnetic field of two electromagnets producing oscillating alternating current. So the ammeter's pointer moves according to the formation and configuration of an elastic magnetic field as a result of the interaction between two "shifting" magnetic fields of two electromagnets inside the ammeter. Generally, all ammeters provide only positive readings, with the smallest measurement being zero.

Nevertheless, assume, for example, that the readings on an ammeter are fluctuating exactly between –2A and 2A from time to time. This does not imply that the exact same number of free/drifting electrons are flowing to and fro along a circuit at one time. No ammeter is sensitive enough to measure the exact number of free/drifting electrons that are flowing through them. In reality, an ammeter is only good for gauging direct current.

Generally, the upper reading and the lower reading of alternating current electricity of an ammeter are hardly exactly the same all the time. Somehow it has become common to assume that the ammeter's reading of an alternating current fluctuates between *a* amps and −*a* amps, as if there is the exact same number of free/drifting electrons at any one time flowing through the ammeter during the time of peak flow. The main reason for this assumption is that some people have made a blatant attempt to validate the absolute process, all the while knowing that the alternating current (AC) is the flow of oscillating alternating current.

Some may argue that an oscilloscope can be used to measure the magnitude of AC current, as an oscilloscope gives a better reading showing that the electric current fluctuates between *a* amps and −*a* amps. Undoubtedly, the push-induced current should be much stronger than the pull-induced current. In contrast, on an oscilloscope's screen, the amplitude of *a* amps and −*a* amps is exactly the same. However, this may not be correct, because the current is produced from a different phase. Remember that push-phase free electrons are laden with an abundance of stationary photons, whereas pull-phase drifting electrons are not packed with stationary photons. Therefore, the absolute of both the positive peaks and the negative peaks of alternating current should be hardly the same given the complexity of their respective flow and interactions. Most likely, an oscilloscope is not sensitive enough to detect any differences in strength between push-induced and pull-induced currents, in which a push-induced current should be much stronger than the absolute value of a pull-induced current.

In addition, push-induced free electrons are much more massive in terms of their content simply because they possess more stationary photons. Thus, they have a greater momentum than does the pull-induced current. Push-induced free electrons are more sustainable, since they are able to travel a long distance, whereas pull-induced free electrons can only travel a much shorter distance, as they possess less momentum. Push-induced free electrons are produced in droves by the transformer; therefore, push-induced free electrons are surrounded by a more strenuous magnetic field than are pull-induced "drifting" electrons. Some may argue that the same number of pull-induced free electrons would be produced to balance out with the total number of push-induced free electrons generated by the transformer. Since metallic atoms' orbitals overlap to a greater extent than do the atoms of insulators and semiconductors, we can confidently say that the number of drifting electrons produced during the pull-induced process is much smaller than the number of push-induced free electrons that are so produced. If metallic atoms lose a few free electrons, this might not lead to a serious decrease in their atomic size and will not trigger the immediate need to induce the pull process (keep in mind the assumption that the absolute charge of an electron is much weaker than that of a proton). Furthermore, the orbitals of all metallic atoms overlap to a greater extent, which means that they are not very sensitive to losing a number of stationary electrons. Thus, a transformer's push-induced process does not necessarily lead to the production of the exact same number of drifting electrons during the pull-induced process. In addition, the sinuous graph of alternating current that appears on an oscilloscope like a smooth curve does not present a true picture of the complex flow of oscillating current. The reading of the alternating current flowing within a cable should not resemble a perfectly smooth sinuous curve because interactions and interferences among push-phase free electrons and stationary electrons, and interactions among drifting electrons and stationary electrons, are by no means necessarily smooth. This indirectly implies that the oscilloscope fails to represent the free flow of alternating current without error or inaccuracies. Furthermore, the absolute values of the maximum and minimum of alternating current may not be exactly the same in view of the complexity of the flow. Needless to say, it is naïve to believe that there is the exact same number of free/drifting electrons flowing alternatively in any direction at any one time.

One would argue that absolute process is fit for depicting the flow of an alternating electric current because all free/drifting electrons are, after all, the same as one another – except the direction in which they flow is different from time to time. It is not as simple as that. Just assume that there are two groups, each having the same number of free electrons and each possessing a similar number of photons, but each of these have different flow directions. Wouldn't these two fluxes of free electrons be the same? The different configurations of the magnetic field of current that has been "constructed" by the specific flow of free electrons in different directions reminds us that these two fluxes of free electrons are different from each other simply because their flows are different from one another. It is not just the number of stationary photons or free/drifting electrons that matters. The flow direction of free/drifting electrons matters more. Actually, free electrons with a similar number of photons should not be seen as being much different from one another, but the different configuration of the magnetic field of different current (such as alternating current) at different times proves that our logic is wrong. In a nutshell, free electrons may be different from stationary electrons simply because the number of photons they contain is different. Their direction of flow can also make them different.

Some quantum scientists strongly believe that different magnetic polarities of alternating current per time emerge simply because electrons possess two different and distinctive spins. In other words, all electrons can be divided into two distinct groups, where each type of electron has a different and distinct intrinsic spin. Therefore, the electrons that have a different intrinsic spin help us to define the two magnetic polarities of electrons. The author believes that negatively charged electrons cannot be classified as two distinctive types according to their intrinsic spin. This is because *all* free electrons that are emitted from an electron gun in a cathode ray tube are deflected by a pair of fixed electromagnets and move to a particular spot, as shown at the left of Figure 4. There is only a single spark that appears on the fluorescent screen to indicate where all the electron beams from the electron gun will "land". If it were correct that all electrons are one of two particular types according to their two distinct intrinsic spins, then the free electrons from an electron gun would form two distinct electron beams, as the different orientation of the free electrons' magnetic field would interact differently with the external magnetic field of a pair of fixed-polarity electromagnets, and incidentally the electrons' beam would split into two rays, with two bright spots likely appearing on the fluorescent screen of the cathode ray tube, as shown at the right of Figure 4. In conclusion, unlike what is claimed by quantum scientists, all electrons possess only one unique intrinsic spin.

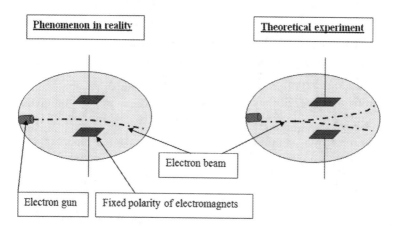

The previous assertion is based on the assumption that the different intrinsic spin of a charged particle, such as a free electron, will have different magnetic polarity. In the example above, all electrons will land on the same spot on the fluorescent screen, which indirectly implies that all electrons must have only one unique intrinsic spin. Somehow all electrons have a similar intrinsic direction of spin; thus, all electrons possess a similar orientation in their magnetic field. But there are electrons that spin in the opposite direction from free electrons; these are called positrons. Positrons always flow in the opposite direction of free electrons because they have a magnetic polarity opposite that of free electrons. We believe that positrons are not as abundant as electrons. In addition, positrons can hardly gain access to a cathode ray tube. Because of this, a cathode ray tube always fails to detect the presence of positrons. In conclusion, electrons and positrons have a similar mass and a similar charge, but they have different intrinsic spinning directions.

It is true that electrons and positrons have unique intrinsic spinning directions when their magnetic polarity is fixed. What is more important to realize is that a specific direction of flow of electric current along a circuit determines the configuration and polarity of the magnetic field that envelops it. The superimposition of the magnetic field of the (majority) free electrons that flow in a particular direction in a circuit shapes the orientation and configuration of the magnetic field along the circuit. This indirectly implies that the flow direction of free electrons along a circuit (keep in mind that the unique shape of the circuit also moulds the configuration of a particular magnetic field along the circuit) determines the configuration and polarity of the magnetic field.

The pointer of a compass flicks vigorously from time to time after the switch has been closed, as shown in Figure 5. This takes place after an elastic magnetic field is formed. The magnetic fields of a compass's pointer and the alternating current electric that is carried along the circuit are "superimposed" on each other. When an elastic magnetic field attempts to loosen its tension, this causes the pointer of the compass to flick. This experimental phenomenon strongly suggests that the direction of flow of the free electrons dictates the orientation and configuration of the magnetic field that forms along a circuit, as every time the current alters its flow direction, the pointer of the compass flicks to a new position. Despite the possibility that electrons and positrons possess a similar number of photons, they, if they have different flow directions, are different from each other in terms of magnetic orientation and configuration;

therefore, they always flow in opposite directions from each other. In a cloud chamber with a fixed external magnetic field, positrons drift along tracks that are opposite from the electrons' tracks because positrons have a magnetic configuration that is opposite to that of electrons. This is due to the fact that positrons spin in the opposite direction of electrons. It is not true that positrons are positively charged particles.

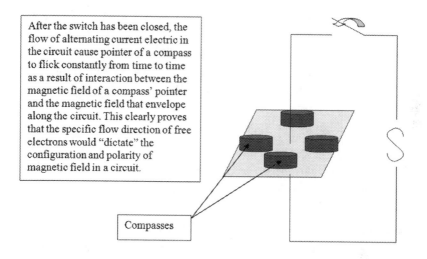

After the switch has been closed, the flow of alternating current electric in the circuit cause pointer of a compass to flick constantly from time to time as a result of interaction between the magnetic field of a compass' pointer and the magnetic field that envelope along the circuit. This clearly proves that the specific flow direction of free electrons would "dictate" the configuration and polarity of magnetic field in a circuit.

Compasses

In addition, along the circuit where alternating current is flowing through, and where the change in configuration of the magnetic field that envelops it strongly suggests that the changed configuration is the result of the superimposition of individual free electrons, the magnetic field of the free electrons is much more dominant than the magnetic field of the positrons. This proves that electrons are much more abundant than positrons. The majority of the free electrons that flow in a particular direction at any one time are those that have been produced in a transformer during the push phase. This leads us to conclude that the free/drifting electrons of an alternating electrical current that flow along a circuit in different directions at different times should be treated distinctively, solely based on their direction of flow. So, a majority flow of free electrons when an oscilloscope registers $\approx a$ amps should be treated as different from the other majority flow of drifting electrons when the oscilloscope registers $\approx -a$ amps, since a specific flow direction of free/drifting electrons dictates the specific orientation and configuration of the magnetic field that envelops those free/drifting electrons. In reality, those free electrons in an alternating current are oscillating in a wire as an abundance of free electrons rushing in one direction before the other drifting electrons, myriad in number, begin dashing in the opposite direction. Of course, there is always a sizeable collection of positrons that constantly flow in the opposite direction of the majority free electrons. In addition, a big flux of strong push-phase free electrons that are squeezing along a copper wire would likely bump into some of the copper atoms' stationary electrons too. In some cases, some free electrons might be forced to change their direction of flow upon impact with these stationary electrons. Undoubtedly, some of the copper atoms' stationary electrons are ejected as drifting electrons, but these types of drifting electrons are not sustainable because their momentum is rather weak. This indirectly creates an unbalanced distribution of charge within the copper atoms, which further complicates the smooth flow of pull-phase electrons.

Imagine that some push-phase free electrons in a very long transmission cable that have travelled a long distance slow down after losing their momentum (a result of the dissipation of the abundance of stationary photons) before transforming into stationary electrons. These electrons will likely be shovelled by next phase of push-phase free electrons. Of course, push-phase free electrons are also attracted to copper atoms, which have an unbalanced distribution of charge. Since the momentum of push-phase free electrons is stronger, these electrons tend to continue to flow past the unbalanced orbital with ease. When slow-moving drifting electrons (the direction of motion of the drifting electrons depends on the whereabouts of copper atoms that have an unbalanced distribution of charge) bump into push-phase free electrons, there is a great chance that the former will cause the latter to divert their direction of flow within the narrow conduit of a copper wire. Under a microscope, a cross section of copper wire looks like a gigantic water pipe. Drifting electrons might not necessarily drift forward. They might transverse diagonally or cross-sectionally, depending on the distribution and whereabouts of the copper atoms that have an unbalanced distribution of charge. Drifting electrons are attracted to these spots. In addition, pull-phase drifting electrons likely interact with stationary electrons, which furthers complicate the free flow of drifting electrons.

Useful applications of the absolute process are limited. Even the most common of these applications, namely comparing the real image of an object to its virtual image in a mirror, is not completely correct. This is because an object is real whereas its mirror image is virtual. Furthermore, the two images are not exactly the same. Because of this, the symbol for "approximately equal to" (≈) should be used instead of the symbol for "equal to" (=), to emphasize that the real object is not the same as its virtual image. Care should be exercised when placing an equals sign (=) in the middle of an equation. This is mainly because the equals sign stresses that what appears on the left-hand side of an equation and what appears on the right-hand side of an equation are exactly the same, just like the balanced level of a chemical balance, where the weight of the item(s) in the left-hand dish is exactly the same as the weight of the item(s) in the right-hand dish. The other common application of absolute process is to indicate that the flow of free electrons in a circuit is not without error. The flow of free electrons (i.e. electrons that contain excess stationary photons and that therefore possess higher momentum. These electrons are able to "migrate" from atom to atom) in the push phase and the flow of drifting electrons during the pull phase should be treated as distinct from each other since the different flow direction of the free/drifting electrons occasions a distinct orientation and configuration of the magnetic field. In a nutshell, there are two important factors that distinguish electrons from one another: the accompanying number of photons and their direction of flow. The different flow direction of free/drifting electrons should be understood as being different simply because the magnetic field enveloping the circuit is different depending on the current's direction of flow. In addition, drifting electrons are enveloped by a much weaker magnetic field than free electrons are. Lastly, absolute process is purely a mathematical concept that is not even fit for describing certain natural phenomena like alternating current, or an object and its mirror image.

Numerical System

Regardless of the numerical system we choose to use for counting, we must first establish a standard of comparison, which is known as the unity. We must have a standard of reference so that we may use it when counting. For instance, when we want to count the number of apples in a basket, we must first identify a particular apple as the unity. Then we make believe that all the apples in the basket are identical to the unity, regardless of the numerical system we choose to use for the counting.

If there are eighteen apples in the basket, regardless of the numerical system we use for the counting, then the sum of our counting should be the same, that is, eighteen apples altogether. To demonstrate that this is so, first we use the binary system to count the basketful of eighteen apples. The sum would be 10010_2 apples. Table 1 shows the counting of a basketful of eighteen apples by using the binary system.

1_{10}	1_2	7_{10}	111_2	13_{10}	1101_2
2_{10}	10_2	8_{10}	1000_2	14_{10}	1110_2
3_{10}	11_2	9_{10}	1001_2	15_{10}	1111_2
4_{10}	100_2	10_{10}	1010_2	16_{10}	10000_2
5_{10}	101_2	11_{10}	1011_2	17_{10}	10001_2
6_{10}	110_2	12_{10}	1100_2	18_{10}	10010_2

In another example, we use a system of counting based on three for a basketful of eighteen apples, as shown in Table 2.

1_{10}	1_3	7_{10}	21_3	13_{10}	111_3
2_{10}	2_3	8_{10}	22_3	14_{10}	112_3
3_{10}	10_3	9_{10}	100_3	15_{10}	120_3
4_{10}	11_3	10_{10}	101_3	16_{10}	121_3
5_{10}	12_3	11_{10}	102_3	17_{10}	122_3
6_{10}	20_3	12_{10}	110_3	18_{10}	200_3

Obviously, different numerical systems limit the quantity of different numbers used to represent objects in the counting. For instance, a system based on three would use permutations of the three lowest whole numbers, namely zero (0), one (1), and two (2). The binary system, on the other hand, uses only permutations of either one (1) or zero (0) to represent different numbers. Both of these examples prove that all numerical systems are compatible with one another. Whether we are using a binary system or a system based on three, the answer is the same, that is, eighteen apples in the basket, although different numerical systems represent this in different ways, such as 10010_2 and 200_3.

When we are counting something, we fall into the habit of thinking that only numbers are involved. Unconsciously we always leave out the unit – in this case, the apple – of what we are counting. We are not counting oranges, are we? Furthermore, before we start counting those apples, we should define the unity first, which is a standard apple. Thereafter, all apples in the basket are assumed to be exactly identical to one another.

A unity consists of two entities. The first of these is the number one (1). The other entity of a unity is its corresponding unit. Apple is the unit of counting in the example above, and all the apples are assumed to be identical to the unity.

The numerical system for counting based on ten was invented by humankind thousands of years ago. Regardless of the language used when counting with a numerical system based on ten, the sums all work out to be exactly the same. In this section, we will analyse the ancient Chinese numerical system based on ten. Like any other peoples, the Chinese use nine distinct numbers to represent what is being counted. These nine distinct numbers are 壹, 贰, 叁, 肆, 伍, 陆, 柒, 捌, and 玖, which are equivalent to the Arabic numerals 1, 2, 3, 4, 5, 6, 7, 8, and 9. In addition, *sire*（十）, *byee*（百）, *jenn* （千）, and *wan* （万）are used to signify ten (10), one hundred (100), one thousand (1,000), and ten thousand (10,000) respectively.

Undoubtedly, ancient Chinese people used the abacus to do simple computations. An abacus has at least seven rows. Each of these rows has seven beads strung together on a bamboo stick. Two beads on the top portion of an abacus are separated by a horizontal piece of wood from five other beads on the lower portion of the abacus. Each of the top portion's beads signifies five units. Each bead on the lower portion of the abacus equals one unit. When the total number of beads on a single bamboo stick is equal to ten, the process is carried forward by one unit to the next higher digit. For instance, take six plus seven, in which six is represented by one upper bead and one lower bead, and seven is represented by one upper bead and two upper beads. Altogether there are two upper beads and three lower beads. Two upper beads transfer to the next higher digit, leaving behind three lower beads. Therefore, six plus seven equals thirteen, which is represented by one lower bead on the next higher digit with three lower beads remaining on the same digit, as shown in Figure 6.

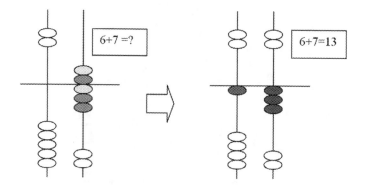

Please refer to Figure 7. It is an early print of an abacus, from the Suan Fa Thung Tsung manuscript, 1593. Focus on the portion of the diagram that is marked with a red circle. Every bamboo stick is given a distinct name. In Figure 7, the smallest digit is on the far right-hand side of the abacus, and the highest digit is on the far left-hand side. The leftmost digit is called *fhun* (分), which is followed by *chien* (钱), *liang* (両), *sire*, *byee*, *jenn*, and *wan*, the last of which is the highest digit in the example. There are different names in Chinese for other numbers that are greater than *wan*. Literally, fhun is a measurement of weight; ten units of fhun equal one chien, and ten chiens make one liang. In ancient China, the liang was almost equivalent to the English ounce and was widely used to measure the weight of gold or silver coins. Liang was the unity used in the Chinese numerical system for gauging collected wealth. On the other hand, *sire*, *byee*, *jenn*, and *wan* — which, remember, indicate ten, one hundred, one thousand, and ten thousand respectively — are basically numbers that signify different magnitudes.

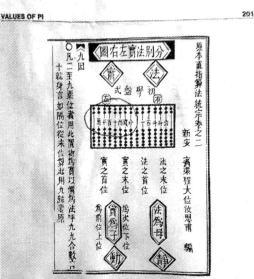

An early printed picture of the abacus, from the Suan Fa Thung Tsung, *1593. (Reproduced from J. Needham, 1959, Vol. 3, p. 76.)*

to lighten manipulations of fractions. In a first-century commentary on the *Nine Chapters*, for example, we find the use of the now familiar rules for square and cube roots, equivalent to $\sqrt{a} = \sqrt{100a}/10$ and $\sqrt[3]{a} = \sqrt[3]{1000a}/10$, which facilitate the decimalization of root extractions.

The idea of negative numbers seems not to have occasioned much difficulty for the Chinese since with two sets of rods—a red set for positive coefficients or numbers and a black set for negatives. Nevertheless, they did not accept the notion that a negative number might be a solution of an equation.

A bead on the right-hand side of a particular bead which is its next higher digit is ten times bigger than itself. This is because the ten beads that are similar in number to the first bead are carried forward by one unit to the next higher digit. This is basically how ancient Chinese people used the abacus for making computations. Ancient Chinese people did not trouble themselves with the existence or non-existence of the zero power. They didn't bother to find out the value of zero power, and yet they were still able to make computations without any errors. They didn't have to worry about the definition of negative power because a bead that is located to the right of another bead always signifies a number ten times bigger.

Which digit on an abacus represents the unity? Undoubtedly, one liang is the unity, as the unit liang (両) was the standard measurement of weight used for either gold or silver coins in ancient China. Ten liangs, or 十両, is one *sire* liang, where *sire* literally means "ten" and liang is the unity. On the other hand, a bead that signifies a number that is two digits larger than the unity is called ten *sires* (十十) or a <u>byee</u>, which literally means that the number is a hundred times bigger than the unity. In addition, a bead that is three digits or four digits greater than the unity, which amounts to ten byees (十百) and ten jenns (十千) respectively, are commonly named a jenn (千; one thousand) and a *wan* (万; ten thousand) respectively, whereas the unit that goes along with them is liang, which is the unity. On the other hand, a bead that is located on the left-hand side of the unity indicates a number ten times smaller than the unity; thus, ten chiens (十钱) are equal to one liang (壹両). And a bead that is two digits to the left-hand side of the unity is one fhun, or 壹分, where ten fhuns (十分) are equal to one chien (壹钱), which literally means that the chien is one hundred times smaller than the unity. By the same token, *sire* liang (十両) is ten times bigger than the unity, and a chien (壹钱) is ten times smaller than the unity, one liang (壹両). Classical Chinese abacus operational philosophy is indeed succinct in defining the numerical system based on ten without incorporating the concept of zero power or negative exponent. The way in which the ancient Chinese people defined the numerical system based on ten with the aid of an abacus has shed doubt on the validity and accuracy of the concept of zero power, negative exponents, and positive exponents.

Most of us were taught to count at a tender age without being reminded of the importance of the unity that should accompany the counting. In a nutshell, we must define the unity first, even before we decide what numerical system we will use for our counting. The unity, which is one plus its corresponding unit, plays a crucial role as the standard of comparison for the items that are being counted. For instance, we identify one particular apple as the standard of comparison, and we then assume that all the apples that we are going to count are exactly identical to the unity in terms of colour, weight, shape, and so forth.

With the unit being a part of whichever numerical system we choose to use, the negative exponent changes the unit from nominator to denominator. Our gut feeling tells us that the definition of a negative exponent can't be accurate for defining any numerical system based on a number that is smaller than the unity, as shown in Figure 8. Similarly, for numbers that are greater than unity, the effect of the positive exponent on the dimension would result in inconsistent units, such as apple^2, as shown in Figure 8, which does not make any sense at all. Presume for a moment that the current definition of zero power is correct, and that the zero power of an apple or the unity must be equal to one only, simply because the zero power of anything becomes one. This is truly absurd, because the unit has vanished. It is bizarre that the unity has been reduced to being dimensionless after the manipulation of the zero power. Since different digits have different unit(s), it is impossible to add them together. This strongly suggests that using positive exponent, negative exponent, and zero power leads to a patently incorrect definition of the numerical system. On the other hand, the zero power of any *thing* should not equal one (1) because only a vacuum, or emptiness, has the dimension of zero. Therefore, the zero power of any number along with its unit must equal zero, or a vacuum, rather than be equal to one. These explanations prompt us to rethink the validity of the definitions of zero power, negative power, and positive exponent. Modern mathematicians probably explain the numerical system in a wrong way by incorporating zero power, positive exponent, and negative exponent.

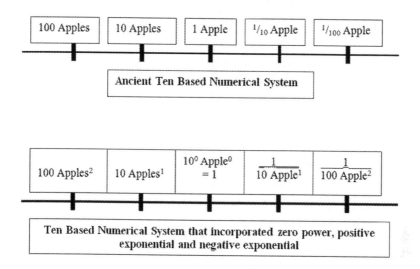

Regardless of any numerical system that we choose for counting something, we must first define the unity. This is so that all numerical systems have a common reference, namely the number one plus its respective unit. Unfortunately, modern mathematicians have mistaken the unity for zero power. They believe that the zero power of any number must be equal to one and that, therefore, all numerical systems merge at one. Unfortunately, this leads modern mathematicians to believe that the zero power of any number is equal to one. Undoubtedly, the zero power is an inaccurate mathematical concept since, by adopting the zero power, the unity vanishes (i.e. becomes dimensionless), which is rather absurd.

In conclusion, before we start counting anything, we must define the unity, which is our standard of comparison, to provide a reference. The unity is made up of the number one plus its corresponding unit, like liang (a standard Chinese ounce, commonly used to measure the weight of gold or silver coins in ancient times). Next, we must decide what numerical system we will use for our counting, such as the binary system or the numerical system based on ten. Counting numbers in ancient times did not require mathematical concepts better suited to rocket science, such as zero power, positive exponent, and negative exponent. The concepts and definitions of zero power, positive exponent, and negative exponent, because of the errors in logic they are based on, have turned out to be useless for explaining the numerical system based on ten. For instance, it is logical to believe that only a vacuum, or emptiness, has a dimension of zero. On the other hand, a negative exponent changes a unit from a nominator to a denominator. Furthermore, the corresponding units for numbers that are greater than the unity are not consistent, such as apple^2, apple^3, and so forth. These logic errors force us to rethink the validity of zero power, positive exponent, and negative exponent in defining any numerical system. Since the concepts of zero power, positive exponent, and negative exponent are defective, the outcomes of computations that use logarithms are never accurate!

Positive and Negative Integral Exponents

When there are n variables of a multiplied together, we denote the product as a^n, which is referred to as "a to the power of n".

$$.a.a.a.a.a.a \ldots \ldots \ldots \ldots \ldots \ldots a = a^n$$

We could count the total number of variable a, which is n number of variable a. Obviously, n is a positive number. Similarly, n, a real number, multiplied by an a variable equals a to the power of n, or a^n.

When n is a negative number, as if this implies that when we count the total number of a we get as a sum a negative number with an exponent, this signifies that we are counting something that is virtual or imaginary. Indirectly, this means there is an imaginary n number of a that is multiplying exponentially. Undoubtedly, the outcome of the computation of a to the power of $-n$ is exactly same as when n is positive, except the outcome of the computation of a^{-n} is virtual (or imaginary) rather than real. The mathematical logic of the negative exponent is the author's own interpretation.

According to modern mathematics, a^{-n} equals $1/a^n$. The error in logic of this negative exponent is that the unit flips from nominator to denominator. This is a very serious error in logic, one that undermines the validity of modern mathematics' definition of a negative exponent. Absolutely no tangible object exists that has a dimensionless dimension over a particular unit, such as $1/$apple, $1/$apple^2, and so forth.

In conclusion, it is certain that modern mathematics' definition of a negative exponent is wrong. We must adopt a new mindset, one that assumes that any mathematical computation involves more than numbers alone. We also need to include the unit. Modern mathematics does not account for the unit of a negative exponent.

When three instances of $-a$ are multiplied together, the product can be expressed as $-a^3$. It can also be expressed as "a to the power of -3", or a^{-3}.

$$(-a)\,(-a)\,(-a) = -a^3 = a^{-3}$$

In conclusion, the author's earlier interpretation of the negative exponent a^{-n}, in which the negative exponent signifies something imaginary that is multiplied by itself n times, could turn out to be correct. Dreamed-up objects are not able to be quantified because they are like a vacuum, or emptiness.

Positive Whole Number of Integral Exponents

We live in three-dimensional physical world. Some may argue that it is more proper to say that we live in a four-dimensional world, the fourth dimension being time. We must understand the real definition of time in parallel with the dynamic state of the universe before we accept the fact that we are dealing only with the physical three-dimensional world. The invisible concept of time cannot be considered as another dimension because we have no control over time. If we construe the time dimension as being like any one of the physical three dimensions, then we conclude that it is feasible for a person to travel along an invisible timeline in the same way he or she moves within the physical world. This is why some quantum scientists have postulated that humankind will be able to engage in time travel if a time machine is invented. The reality is that time travel is only possible in science fiction since we have no control over the dynamic state of the universe.

According to the author, the universe will remain in existence as long as it continues to expand from the effects of the Big Bang explosion. Once the universe reaches its maximum size, it will implode on account of the mutually attracting force of gravity. Then, when all fast-moving celestial objects meet again at the centre of the universe, their impacts will pave the way for the Big Bang explosion. Again, all celestial objects will be flung outwards as the universe starts to expand again until it reaches its maximum size and then implodes again before the imminent big explosion occurs. It is a continuous cycle that the universe will go through endlessly. Of course, life forms emerge at certain places in the universe when the conditions are able to sustain living beings. All life forms will vanish just before or after the next Big Bang because the environment will be too hot and too volatile to sustain life. When the universe has inflated almost to its maximum size, most of its kinetic energy will be transformed into universal gravitational potential energy; subsequently, photons will be exchanged (according to their rate of dissipation and absorption) at minimum levels, as atoms and molecules will seek out stationary photons. Therefore, life forms will cease to exist within the universe well before the universe reaches its maximum size. In some cases, life forms within a particular galaxy will vanish much earlier, after their closest sun has burnt out.

Why do life forms exist? The only plausible explanation is that God created all life forms, including humankind. Scientific knowledge can explain how life forms exist only to a certain extent. For instance, chlorophyll is extremely important to plants for manufacturing food. Biologists still do not fully understand how plants produce chlorophyll. Our understanding of the flora and fauna that exist on earth – especially the flora and fauna that live deep within the ocean – is still limited.

Various timepieces have been invented by humankind to help register the chronological development of any events that take place mainly on earth. Basically, we have a rigid definition of time. For instance, we commonly believe that the duration of every second is the same, as if one second a million years ago were exactly the same as a second in real time. At different dynamic stages of the universe, atoms possess different levels of kinetic energy. The number of stationary photons atoms have also differs at different stages. These photons affect the strength of their nucleons' angular momentum, which in turn controls their unique nucleus structure. Of course, the unique nucleus structure governs the size, configuration, and shape of a unique orbital, which in turn determines the substance's chemical properties and characteristics. To a certain extent, the unique nucleus structure also governs the physical characteristics of an element or its compound(s). Therefore, all elements and compounds should have different but unique physical and chemical characteristics and properties at different dynamic stages of the universe. These characteristics in turn should govern the outcome of the chemical reactions as well as their reaction rates, which indirectly govern the life span of any organism. This hints at the idea that all physical aspects and chemical reactions of any organism are subject to constant adaptation in parallel with the dynamic state of universe. Indirectly, this hints at the idea that the life span of each specific life form is different depending on the dynamic state of the universe. Therefore, the duration of one second for a life form a million years ago would seem to be different from the duration of one second of real time today. The focus is not entirely on the duration of a second but is also on how we *perceive* that duration. For instance, life expectancy was much lower in the eighteenth century than it is now. Therefore, one second centuries ago was perceived to be very fast because of the much shorter life expectancy as compared to the life expectancy nowadays. Of course, better nutrition, a cleaner water supply, better health care, and improved sanitation have made it possible for people to have a longer life expectancy now compared to the life expectancy several centuries ago. But biochemical rates within a biological being should also be different now as compared to the biochemical rates of biological beings several centuries ago. Therefore, one's perception of a second's duration now should be different from a person's perception of a second several centuries ago. Unfortunately there aren't any scientific data to substantiate our claim that one second many centuries ago and one second in real time are perceived as different from one another.

All anthropological and historical data about ancient civilizations are inaccurate. This is mainly because the method of carbon dating is not without errors. The author strongly believes that even radioactive substances' rates of decay have not been spared from modification in parallel to the different dynamic state of the universe. In other words, the half-life of any particular radioactive substance is never a constant mainly because various denominations of nucleons' energy are subject to changes in parallel to the different dynamic state of the universe. Similarly, the number of stationary photons on the nucleons of a particular radioactive substance will be different when the dynamic state of the universe is different. This affects especially the strength of the nucleons' angular momentum. The strength of the angular momentum of nucleons plays an important role in ensuring the stability of the unique nucleus structure of a particular radioactive substance, which in turn determines the duration of its corresponding half-life. Thus, its half-life is subject to modification in parallel to the dynamic state of the universe.

The modern definition and measurement of time are "accurate" for a specific period of time. For instance, the duration of one second one million years ago might not be the same as the duration of one second in real time. The author reckons that the definition of time would be meaningful only after we were able to use a more systematic approach and had invented reliable clocks to gauge time. We don't know exactly when the sun will eventually cease burning. Furthermore, the sun may "die" early, long before the universe expands to its maximum size, which would make all life forms perish because, with a dead sun, no chemical reactions could take place and the environment would be too volatile for sustaining life. The author defines a univperiod as a period of time referring either to the duration between the Big Bang and the expansion of the universe to its maximum size or the duration when the universe implodes before the second Big Bang takes place. All life forms including human being emerge and vanish within each individual univperiod. According to astronomical observations, the universe is in an expanding phase in real time. The flow of time is only a description of the dynamic state of the universe. If we understand this reasoning, then it is clear to us that we are not really living in a four-dimensional world, as widely believed by most modern scientists, simply because we have *no* control of the dynamism of the universe. Time is definitely not another (invisible) dimension. The real world consists of only three dimensions. Therefore, travelling through time to the past or the future is only sci-fi after all.

Since we live in a three-dimensional physical world without a fourth dimension, all applications of mathematical philosophy should reflect this reality. If we have been asked to represent one metre to the power of 0.3, (1 metre)$^{0.3}$, some of us would be sure that the answer is 1 metre$^{0.3}$. It seems to be correct, but the unit metre$^{0.3}$ does not make sense at all. To have 0.3 dimensions of a metre is not feasible in reality; therefore, such an attempt is undefined. In a nutshell, any mathematical computation must do more than justify itself in terms of quantity only. Its respective unit must also make sense. Both the number and its unit must be logical in order to be acceptable.

The example above suggests that the positive exponent is a valid operation if the exponents are positive whole numbers only. For instance, a^n is valid if n is a whole number. If n is a real number, such as 0.3, then we see that metre$^{0.3}$ does not exist in the real (physical) world. There is no way we can describe metre$^{0.3}$ in the real world. In short, only positive whole-number exponents are considered to be valid in describing the physical world. A real number of integral exponents is not valid when describing the physical world. In addition, an integral number with a negative power is in violation of logic. Just assume that the modern definition of a negative exponent is correct and that the negative exponent, first a nominator, becomes the denominator. This is a serious violation of mathematical logic. As indicated in the previous section, "Positive and Negative Integral Exponents", one would only have a negative exponent after multiplying imaginary objects. Then again, the product of a computation involving any object in terms of its quantity and unit that turns out to be a negative exponent obviously indicates that the object is imaginary, like a vacuum; therefore, those negative integral exponents have little usefulness or meaning.

Modern mathematics' definitions of negative exponents and (real) positive exponents are invalid, as they fail to align with reality. The concept of logarithm manipulation, a technique that is built on these defective mathematical concepts, validates the real number of an integral exponent; therefore, the outcome of a computation involving the application of a logarithm is never accurate. As a matter of fact, the outcome of a computation using a logarithm is only approximate to the true answer. If the real numbers of integral exponents were mathematically valid, then answers derived from mathematical manipulation based on a logarithm would be 100 per cent accurate.

Since a computer is more accurate than a logarithm, nowadays engineers and scientists do not rely on logarithms when performing their computations. The author stresses that the computer is not perfect either. Computers do not necessarily produce a 100 per cent accurate answer every time because a computer chip's circuit has its limitations. The answer to a math problem provided by a computer will not be accurate when the input or output is beyond the computer's ability to process. Even if the computation is impossible to carry out, the computer will confidently provide an answer as if the answer exists and is deemed to be correct. For instance, the square root of two ($\sqrt{2}$) is an irrational number, which indirectly implies that there is no a single number that, when multiplied by itself twice, will equal exactly two without rounding up or down. In other words, there is no answer for the square root of two. On the other hand, a computer will provide you with an answer for the square root of two as if it were correct to many decimal places. If a computation is of the utmost importance, the author suggests that a person do the computation manually to ensure accuracy. We just can't put 100 per cent of our trust in a computer.

Radical Notation

Since positive whole number integral exponents only are considered to be valid, the nth root for a number of a must be expressed as $n\sqrt{a}$ rather than as $a^{1/n}$. This is mainly because $1/n$ is a real number. In addition, the expression of $n\sqrt{a}$ implies that a number multiplying itself n times will equal a. Similarly, the expression $a^{m/n}$ should be stated as $\sqrt[n]{a^m}$ because m/n is a real number too. Either n or m's operation could be done first without affecting the outcome of the computation. For instance, an expression of $2\sqrt{4^3}$, where the square root operation proceeds first, would reduce to 2^3, which equates to eight (8). Similarly, if 4^3 proceeds first, it will equal sixty-four (64). Then, the square root of sixty-four ($\sqrt{64}$) equals eight again. This example clearly proves that either n or m's operation can proceed first without jeopardizing the outcome of the computations. This example focuses only on the numeral aspect of the computation. If units are also involved, then the interpretation of units in the calculations will be different depending on which operation is carried out first. For instance, if the calculation of the square root is carried out first, the unit attached to four could be simply apples, with the square root of four apples being an attempt to figure out how many apples there are per row if they have been arranged in the shape of a cube. Obviously, the answer would be two apples per row. Then, we will find the number of apples in the cube, wherein there are two apples per dimension. Of course, there are eight apples altogether in the cube. On the other hand, if the cube exponent proceeds first, then the unit attached to four will be apples per dimension. The cube with a dimension of four apples per row will have sixty-four apples in it. Arrange these sixty-four apples in a square. Of course, there will be eight apples per row. Pay attention to the units. The author explains these examples as if the units involved are not rigid, as units have somehow been skewed to accommodate the explanation of mathematical operations in order to keep mathematical operations sound and logical. The units that are set in a mathematical problem likely determine the logical algorithm, namely which mathematical operations come first and which ones proceed later.

In conclusion, we are living in a finite three-dimensional world; therefore, an exponent to power m/n, in which m/n turns out to be a real number, clashes with basic mathematical logic. Mathematical logic must always comply with the physical world. Mathematical concepts and the real world must always complement each other. Take for instance a mathematical operation where the units involved are (a apple/row)$^{3/2}$. It could be simplified to (a apple/row)$^{1.5}$, which makes no physical sense at all. Of course, the units that are involved should be treated with flexibility. Obviously, (a apple/row)^3 is a mathematical operation meant to quantify the number of apples that are arranged in the form of a cube, where each side has a number of apples per row. Apparently, the unit of the outcome would be cubic apples and not apple^3/row^3, where the nominator's unit row[3] would vanish to become cubic. Subsequently, those apples would be arranged in the form of a two-dimensional square for a mathematical operation of $\sqrt{(a^3}$ apple/cube). Obviously the cubic nominator could be dropped since it has nothing to do with the square root manipulation. Undoubtedly, the unit of the final outcome of the computation would be apples per row. This very example simply indicates the danger of blindly and rigidly keeping track of the units involved in computations. Sometimes we must apply mathematical logic in order to get the correct unit. The exponent of m/n can normally be simplified and expressed as an equivalent real number which does not align with the dimensions of the physical world, such as (a apple/row)$^{1.5}$. In addition, the negative exponent turns the units from nominators to denominators, which is a serious violation of mathematical logic. Therefore, the existing expression of $a^{m/n}$ should be expressed as $n\sqrt{a^m}$. It is true that mathematical operations that involve both positive exponents and negative exponents can never fuse to become a single operation instead, e.g. (a apple/row)$^{1.5}$.

Function and Its Range of Independent Variables

It is commonly known that a function is a set of ordered pairs made up of two or more different variables. Such variables can be classified as independent variable(s) and a dependent variable. The value of the dependent variable is solely dependent upon the value of the independent variable(s). For instance, a set of ordered pairs consisting of a dependent variable and an independent variable will reflect a relationship between both variables. Furthermore, this will be a unique relationship, one in which every dependent variable is associated with one, and only one, independent variable. Such a description of the relationship between a set of independent variables and a dependent variable is called a function. The subsets of the independent variable are normally defined as being all the real numbers ranging from the negative infinite to the positive infinite.

The author suspects that there is some inappropriateness in defining the range of subsets of the independent variable as a function. All negative values of an independent variable should not necessarily be included as the subsets of the independent variable in order to qualify as a function. According to the author, a feasible range of independent variables is sufficient to qualify an algebraic expression as a function. Thus, the subsets of the independent variable of a function need not necessarily range from negative real infinite to positive real infinite. A range of positive numbers to start with would suffice in defining the range of the independent variable. It is a common practice in the process of collecting data for any form of experiment to define the time as zero, denoting the beginning of the experiment. In another example, the association between electric current and the voltage of an electric circuit can be expressed as $V = IK$, where K is the slope of the graph, voltage versus current, as shown in Figure 9. To be more precise, Ohm recognized that the value for K should equal the value of a resistor in the circuit provided that there is no rise in temperature on account of the resistance.

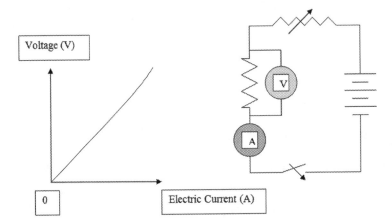

No matter how complexly free electrons flow along an electric wire, the relationship between electric current and voltage is summarized in Figure 9. Take note that there is no negative range of electric current supplied in Figure 9. At the outset of the experiment when the switch is opened, no flow of electric current is the very first set of data. This example supports the author's suggestion that the range of independent variables of a function can be applied to a set of positive numbers, including zero and excluding any negative range, and still be considered as valid.

There are not many "pure" functions in the physical world. For most natural phenomena, independent variables do not seem to be strictly associated with a dependent variable as dictated by the form of a simple function, mainly because this is a complex world. Most natural phenomena cannot be expressed as a simple function. For instance, it is commonly believed, as stated by Ohm's law, that electric current correlates with voltage. Ohm's law stresses that current and voltage correlate with one another linearly as long as there is no rise in the temperature of the circuit. Such a condition is unrealistic. Ohm and other scientists of his day lacked an understanding of the complex flow of free electrons in a circuit at the microscopic level. Free electrons have an excess of stationary photons; therefore, they possess higher momentum. They are also more massive, simply because photons are particles. Indirectly, this implies that the free electrons produced in a chemical reaction within a dry cell are loaded with photons. In addition, different types of chemical reactions produce free electrons that are loaded with a different number of stationary photons, with the latter adhering to former. Besides, different types of chemical reactions in different types of batteries produce different numbers of free electrons per time. Therefore, different types of dry cell batteries have different voltage levels (i.e. the rate of production of free electrons) and durability (i.e. the total number of free electrons that are able to be produced).

Obviously, it is the tendency of free electrons to shed the excess stationary photons that have adhered to them to the surrounding area soon after the latter have been produced. Therefore, it is impossible to store up electrical energy. We commonly utilize excess electrical energy in the process of electrolysis to charge a battery, so those free electrons lock in *some* cations before they precipitate on a cathode. When there is a call for electrical energy, those atoms or molecules on the cathode are available to participate in a chemical reaction with electrolytes, and this reaction produces fresh free electrons on the cathode. On the other hand, excess electricity produced by a hydroelectric dam is normally used to pump water from downstream to top up the water level upstream since there is no better way to store up excess electrical energy.

Whenever free electrons are flowing along a conductor, they lose excess stationary photons to the surrounding area. Even if they are flowing through a perfect conductor, free electrons tend to push some stationary photons into the surrounding area, but they shed fewer of these dissipated photons when they are flowing through a resistor. This is because the orbital of a good conductor such as gold is larger in size. Gold atoms overlap one another much more extensively in a conductor than in a resistor. Generally, the orbital size of a conductor is much larger than the orbital size of a resistor. Thus, free electrons shed fewer stationary photons when they are flowing through a good conductor. When free electrons enter the space of atoms/molecules in a resistor, they shed a substantial number of stationary photons to the surrounding area. Undoubtedly, the atoms of a resistor have a smaller atomic size and tend to have smaller orbitals, meaning that there is a shorter distance between the electrons and the nuclei. In addition, the overlapping among orbitals is limited. If it weren't, then it would be more difficult for free electrons to flow through the conductor before being stranded within the resistor. In other words, free electrons that enter the space of an atom inside a resistor emulate the characteristics of the stationary electrons by shedding the abundance of stationary photons to the surrounding area. Subsequently, they are trapped within the resistor. Naturally the temperature of a resistor rises sharply whenever there is an electric current flowing through it. The bottom line is that free electrons shed their stationary photons to the surrounding area whether they are travelling through a perfect conductor or a resistor. Of course, more heat is generated by free electrons when they are flowing through a resistor than when they are flowing through a conductor. Copper wire is considered to be a rather good conductor, but its temperature rises when there is direct current flowing through it. The temperature of either a conductor or a resistor will rise whenever a current is flowing through it. Of course, the resistor rises to a higher temperature than the conductor does.

Without a doubt, the heat generated by the current of free electrons disrupts the free flow of free electrons. A good deal of the heat from dynamic free electrons is absorbed by the resistor's atoms, especially their nuclei; because of this, the temperature of the resistor rises after it is heated up for a sustainable duration. Naturally, the resistor's atoms' nuclei absorb dynamic photons from the free electrons, more than the number of photos that they initially dissipated to the surrounding area. The free electrons start to vibrate agitatedly after they have gained more momentum as a result of absorbing more dynamic photons. This further affects the free flow of free electrons since the extent of the overlap of the orbital among atoms is subject to strain depending on the wobbling of the nuclei. After the temperature of the resistor has risen to a certain degree, the resistor's nuclei increase their rate of exchanging photons after the current flows for a sustainable duration. Subsequently, a small number of free electrons that flow through the resistor absorb a lot more dynamic photons from the nuclei of the resistor than the ones that they dissipate to the surroundings, which leads to the erratic drifting of those free electrons. Changes to the extent of overlapping among orbitals and heightened interaction among free electrons due to backlog cause disruption to the smooth flow of free electrons within the resistor. In other words, when the temperature within a resistor rises significantly, we expect its resistance to increase further. A rise in temperature surely takes place even when a current is flowing through a good conductor at room temperature for a sustainable duration, because free electrons shed photons as they try to emulate those stationary electrons while trying to skip from orbital to orbital; as a result, nuclei increase their wobbling, which in turn affects the extent of overlapping among orbitals, which compromises the smooth flow of free electrons. A higher volume of current flow causes the temperature rise to be even more drastic. In this case, the free flow of electrons along the wire/ resistor is severely disrupted because a bottleneck scenario ensues – the result of too many free electrons trying to squeeze through it. Upgrading the electric circuit so that it has a wire/resistor that is larger in diameter eases the free flow of current and seemingly lowers the resistance of the wire. In such a case, less heat dissipates out from the wire because the extent of the wobbling among nuclei is not that great; subsequently, orbitals still overlap extensively in order to facilitate the continuous flow of free electrons.

On the other hand, at much lower temperatures, nucleons heighten their intrinsic spinning rate after losing a substantial number of stationary photons while transforming more of their angular momentum into magnetic energy as their nuclei are enveloped by strong magnetic fields. Such a phenomenon is called superconductivity. Quantum scientists claim that the resistance in a circuit is zero. This perception is *wrong*. There is no doubt that there is a sustainable flow of free electrons in a circuit. All free electrons that have been freshly produced as a result of the interaction among magnetic fields of nuclei and stationary electrons enhance the ability of the stationary electrons to absorb more dynamic photons from the surrounding area, as the existence of a compact elastic magnetic field on the stationary electrons – a result of the interaction between the magnetic fields of nuclei and their stationary electrons – forcibly makes more stationary photons adhere to stationary electrons before transforming them into free electrons. In addition, those stationary electrons heighten their intrinsic spinning rate; as a result, they are also enveloped by stronger magnetic fields. Subsequently, the presence of stronger magnetic fields enables those stationary electrons to be more effective in amassing dynamic photons from the surrounding area. Like all free electrons, freshly produced free electrons shed a sizeable number of photons to the surrounding area while emulating the stationary electrons of the atoms when entering their orbitals. The atomic size of those atoms is much smaller on account of the extremely low temperatures. Similarly, the extent of overlapping among orbitals is rather extensive as a result of shrinkage on account of low temperatures. Superconductivity does not in any way imply zero resistance or the capability to freshly produce a sizeable number of free electrons continuously as a result of the strong magnetic field enveloping nuclei at an extremely low temperature.

All electrons, free electrons included, are negatively charged particles. Electrons repel each other because there is a repulsive electrostatic force among like-charge particles. When the current is increased to a certain optimum level, a further increase in current causes a disruption in flow. This is because of the bottleneck effect, which likely occurs along the conduit of a circuit when too many free electrons are trying to squeeze through the circuit. Naturally, heat quickly builds up along the circuit in such a case, as an abundance of photons are shed by those squeezing free electrons. Any further increase in the flow of current will lead to a serious disruption in flow as the great number of free electrons are squeezing through. In other words, after an optimum flow of current, any further increase in the flow of current leads to a serious disruption in flow when there are just too many free electrons trying to squeeze through the seemingly narrow conduit of a circuit. This increases the probability that the free electrons will collide with one another violently, thus causing a serious disruption in flow. So, until a certain stage, any further increase in voltage will not necessarily lead to an increase in the flow of current. Any further increase in voltage will cause the flow of current to stagnate, mainly because of the limitation on the physical circuit itself, which will induce the bottleneck condition on the circuit. If we upgrade and use a wire/resistor with a larger diameter, then the congestion eases and any increase in voltage leads to a parallel increase in the flow of current.

In conclusion, Ohm's law is too idealistic. Any flow of electric current results in a rise in temperature along a circuit. Any volume of electric current flow encourages heat to build up along a resistor/wire, which in turn disrupts the smooth flow of free electrons within a circuit. Therefore, Ohm's law is not applicable if a rise in temperature occurs when the electric current is allowed to flow for a sustainable duration or when a huge current flows through the circuit and leads to a bottleneck situation. After an optimum flow of free electrons has been attained, any further increase in voltage may not necessarily lead to a parallel increase in current flow, simply because of the physical limitation of the circuit itself, but a serious disruption to the current flow will occur due to the bottleneck phenomenon within the resistor/wire. Indeed there are not many natural phenomena that can be expressed by perfect functions. Ohm's law does not accurately reflect reality, as it is impossible to resist any rise in temperature within a resistor/wire when electric current is flowing through it, provided for a very short duration. It is time for us to discard the ragged old mindset that all natural phenomena can be described by a simple mathematics equation, as quantum scientists believe. The author stresses that it is more important to be able to fathom the microscopic processes that take place at the atomic level than it is to hope that a simple mathematical equation will be formulated to explain the processes that take place. This is simply because the processes are too complicated to be put into the form of a simple equation.

Inverse Functions

According to modern mathematics, f inverse is the inverse of a function. The ordered pairs of $f^{1}(x)$ are obtained by interchanging the coordinates in each ordered pair of $f(x)$. The denotation of -1 in f^{1} does not represent a negative exponent. Instead, it is merely a symbol for denoting the inverse function.

The author would like to stress the importance of determining the difference between an independent variable and a dependent variable. According to the scientific perspective, the independent variable is usually the one that can hardly be dictated or controlled during an experiment's data collection process. On the other hand, the dependent variable is the one that can be easily obtained, as it corresponds to the independent variable. Because the physical flow of time cannot be dictated or controlled, time is normally treated as the independent variable. Data are collected at specified increments, for instance, every second interval. For every collected dependent variable, the reading corresponding to the specific time frame is considered to be a set of data. The truth about the inverse function is that the distinction between the independent variable and the dependent variable is taken for granted, as if the two were interchangeable.

According to the author, mathematics plays a crucial role in explaining the sensibility of scientific theories. The capability to include both independent and dependent variables in the form of a function to support a possible explanation that can be recognized as a theory would definitely improve our understanding of natural phenomena. In short, mathematics is not a field of its own. Mathematics also applies to the scientific and technological fields, helping to make sense and at the same time enhancing our understanding vis-à-vis the research and development of new scientific knowledge. Then again, this does not imply that all natural phenomena are strictly dictated by some simple mathematical equations, which is something that most quantum scientists believe.

In view of the various unique roles that mathematics is assumed to play, any definition of mathematical concepts must retain its capability and validity when applied to a complementary field, such as engineering or science. The definition of inverse function has violated our need to make a distinction between an independent variable and a dependent variable. Currently, it is as if these two things are interchangeable and can be swapped. This clashes with basic scientific beliefs. Disregarding the need to distinguish an independent variable from a dependent variable in relation to the inverse function has indeed crumbled the logic of scientific world. Therefore, the author stresses that it is important to rethink the validity of the definition of the inverse function.

In Search of Pi (π)

Modern mathematicians believe that pi (π) is an irrational number. We commonly use the formula πr^2 to quantify the area of a circle. If we draw a circle with a radius of two centimetres, we know that the size of that circle is finite. Since π is an irrational number, this implies that the area of such a circle can never be quantified. This observation comes across as a contradiction to the fact that the area of the circle is finite. But the author strongly agrees that the value of π is indeed an irrational number. This is mainly because the arc of a circle is curved. We can quantify the area of a figure with accuracy only when the figure is a square, rectangle, or triangle. When the scale is shrunk (i.e. when the size of a circle is smalled up), there are remnants, especially in the circle's arc, that are left out and unaccounted for in the computations. The scale could shrink forever, yet we would always fail to compute these remnant areas mostly near the arc of a circle. Undoubtedly, it is difficult to quantify the area of a circle with accuracy and precision because a circle's circumference is curved. Assuming that the formula for computing the area of a circle, πr^2, is correct, the value of π should be an irrational number because the scale could shrink forever. Yet there are always remnant areas, especially near the edge of the circle's arc, that cannot be accounted for. Attempts to find a more accurate total area for a circle could go on forever. Therefore, π is an irrational number. Some modern mathematicians suggest that π is equivalent to 22/7. The rationale behind this fraction has not been substantiated by any solid mathematical proof, but it gives us a way to easily memorize the value of π. The author has worked out a systematic way to derive the value of π. Is this mathematical methodology of deriving π correct and proper?

What is the true value of π? Is it 3.141592654 or 22/7? How would it be possible to quantify the true value of π? First, we assume that the formula for quantifying the total area of a circle, πr^2, is correct. Then, we draw a quarter of a circle with a radius of 1 cm on a piece of 180-mm × 260-mm graph paper, with each square measuring 2 mm, as shown in the first computation in the Appendix. We divide this quarter of a circle into seven segments (three right-angled triangles and four rectangles) so that the area of those segments can be computed with minimal errors.

- The area of segment 1 is four 2-mm units × one 2-mm unit, which equals four 2-mm × 2-mm squares.
- The area of segment 2, a right-angled triangle with one 2-mm unit opposite and two 2-mms units adjacent, has an area of one 2-mm × 2-mm square (one 2-mm unit × two 2-mm units).
- Segment 3, which is rectangular in shape with two 2-mm units of width and three 2-mm units of height, has an area of six 2-mm × 2-mm squares.
- Segment 4, which is an isosceles triangle with one 2-mm unit opposite and one 2-mm unit adjacent, has an area of 0.5 (2-mm × 2-mm square).
- Segment 5 is a right-angled triangle with two 2-mm units opposite and one 2-mm unit adjacent. It has an area of ½ (one 2-mm unit × two 2-mm units), which turns out to be one 2-mm × 2-mm square.
- The rectangular segment 6, one 2-mm unit in width and two 2-mm units in height, has an area of two 2-mm × 2-mm squares.
- Segment 7, which is a rectangle of five 2-mm units in length × one 2-mm unit in width, has an area of five 2-mm × 2-mm squares.

The approximate area of a quarter circle with a radius measuring 1 cm is 19.5 2-mm × 2-mm squares, which is the sum of the area for segments 1–7: (4 + 1 + 6 + 0.5 + 1 + 2 + 5) 2-mm × 2-mm squares. The approximate area of a full circle is seventy-eight 2-mm × 2-mm squares, which is derived by multiplying four by 19.5 2-mm × 2-mm squares, since four equal quarters make a complete circle. In addition, five 2-mm units times five 2-mm units, or twenty-five 2-mm × 2-mm squares, is equal to 1 cm². Seventy-eight 2-mm

× 2-mm squares of the area of a circle with a radius of 1 cm multiplied by (1 cm² / twenty-five 2-mm × 2-mm squares) equals 3.12 cm². We are trying to determine the precise value of π, so we assume the formula for computing the total area of a circle, πr², to be correct. The total area of a circle with a radius of 1 cm is π cm²: π × (1 cm)². Based on our graphing the result of our computations of a circle with a radius of 1 cm, the value of π is estimated to be 3.12. This is because the total area of a physical circle with a radius of 1 cm, derived graphically, should equal π.

Next, we draw several quarters of circles with radii of different lengths, such as 2 cm, 3 cm, 4 cm, 5 cm, 6 cm, 7 cm, and 8 cm respectively, on 180-mm × 260-mm graph paper with squares of 2 mm. *All of these* will eventually help us to find the area of a physical circle with a radius of 1 cm. In other words, all quarters of the circle with radii of different lengths actually represent a portion of a physical circle with a radius of 1 cm. The process to find the area of those circles graphically with different radius lengths in cm² is exactly the same as the one we used in the first example. Please refer to the Appendix to see detailed computations of the areas of circles with different radii.

The author wishes there were much bigger sheets of graph paper so that larger quarter circles could be drawn in order to find a better reading for π. The conclusions that are drawn based on the length of the radius, from 1 cm to 8 cm with an increment of 1 cm, may not be conclusive enough.

The results for finding the value of π are summarized in Table 3.

(1) Scale Actual: Drawing	(2) Area 1cm²: # 2mmx2mm squares	(3) Area of quarter of a circle (# 2mmx2mm squares)	(4) Area of a circle (# 2mmx2mm squares) 4 x (3)	(5) Area of a circle (cm²) (4) x (2)	(6) Value of π of a physical 1cm-radius circle (5)=(6)
1cm: 1cm	1: 5x5	19.5	78	3.12	3.12
1cm: 2cm	1: 10x10	80	320	3.2	3.2
1cm: 3cm	1: 15x15	175	700	3.1111111	3.1111111
1cm: 4cm	1: 20x20	311.5	1246	3.115	3.115
1cm: 5cm	1: 25x25	488.5	1954	3.1264	3.1264
1cm: 6cm	1: 30x30	704.375	2817.5	3.130555556	3.130555556
1cm: 7cm	1: 35x35	963.375	3853.5	3.145714286	3.145714286
1cm: 8cm	1: 40x40	1257.375	5029.5	3.1434375	3.1434375

Surprisingly, all the sought values of π are not a constant. Furthermore, those sought values of π are not 3.141592654 … Another important observation is that those sought values of π are constantly fluctuating, first from 3.12 to 3.2

and then to 3.1111111, before settling at 3.115. Later the value surges to 3.1264. Then it increases to 3.130555556 before increasing further to 3.145714286, but eventually it decreases to 3.1434375 as the radii of the drawn quarter circle increase from 1 cm to 8 cm with increments of 1 cm. Our basic assumption is that as the radii of drawn quarter circles get longer, the accuracy in finding the value of π should improve. Furthermore, the values of π should converge to become a specific value. But none of these values is what we get from our limited number of quarter circles with different radius sizes. The best conclusion is that the formula for computing the area of a circle is not πr^2. This means that no perfect formula exists for computing the total area of a circle. The reality is that a formula such as πr^2 is only good for approximating the area of a circle with r radius. The author strongly believes that more research needs to be carried out to ascertain a better formula for computing the area of a circle. We don't know – since we don't have larger sheets of graph paper on which to draw much larger quarter circles – whether the value of π would eventually converge or not. Humankind has been puzzling over the value of π for centuries. Now we are not so sure if the value of π in πr^2 when we are seeking to find the total area of a circle is the same in terms of its value to the formula $2\pi r$ in determining the circle's corresponding circumference. The same applies to the value of π in the formula $\frac{4}{3}\pi r^3$ in determining the volume of a sphere. At the end of the day, π does not turn out to be a special magical number like 3.141592654 … Nor does π equal 22/7, as we used to believe.

Chapter 2

Trigonometry

Pythagorean Theorem and Reality

The Pythagorean theorem tries to determine the relationship of the adjacent side, the opposite side, and the hypotenuse of a right-angled triangle such that the sum of the square of the adjacent and opposite sides is equal to the square of the hypotenuse, as shown in the equation below.

$$(adjacent)^2 + (opposite)^2 = (hypotenuse)^2$$

Is the Pythagorean theorem correct? The author feels that the Pythagorean theorem is not correct. For instance, we can draw a lot of different sizes of right-angled triangles whose adjacent legs have similar lengths. This clearly proves that the measurement of the adjacent leg is completely independent of the measurements of the opposite leg and the hypotenuse. Another important observation is that all these right-angled triangles are unique, which indirectly indicates that the adjacent leg, the opposite leg, and the hypotenuse of any right-angled triangle are not associated with one another as is dictated by the Pythagorean theorem.

According to the Pythagorean theorem, if the lengths of the adjacent and opposite legs of a right-angled triangle are the same, then the triangle's hypotenuse must be $\sqrt{2}$. A 1-1-$\sqrt{2}$ right-angled triangle is shown in Figure 10.

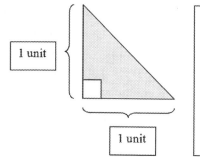

1 unit

1 unit

The hypotenuse of a right angled triangle could always be determined by graphical method. In other words, based on a drawn right angled triangle to scale before measuring its hypotenuse directly to get the magnitude of the hypotenuse with higher accuracy than one that provided by Pythagoras theorem.

The dimensions of the adjacent leg, opposite leg, and hypotenuse of a right-angled triangle as shown in Figure 10 are all finite. Also, all dimensions of the right-angled triangle shown in Figure 10 are fixed. According to the Pythagorean theorem, the hypotenuse of the right-angled triangle is $\sqrt{2}$, which is an irrational number. This implies that $\sqrt{2}$ has an infinite number of decimal places. If we had a ruler with the ability to measure the infinite, we would just need to measure the length of the hypotenuse of the right-angled triangle in Figure 10 once in order to get its reading, mainly because the length of the hypotenuse is fixed. This contradicts what the Pythagorean theorem tells us: that we will never manage to get the measurement of the length of the hypotenuse of the right-angled triangle even if we use a ruler capable of measuring the infinite, simply because $\sqrt{2}$ is an irrational number, as if the hypotenuse will continue to extend outward in defiance of the law of conservation of matter. This example proves without a doubt that the Pythagorean theorem is not logical and does not reflect reality in parallel with the law of conservation of matter. The Pythagorean theorem is only good for estimating the length of the hypotenuse of a right-angled triangle. This implies that the respective lengths of the adjacent leg, opposite leg, and hypotenuse of a right-angled triangle are not strictly associated with each other as dictated by the Pythagorean theorem. Any mathematical concepts or theories that are based on the Pythagorean theorem, such as trigonometric identities, would be automatically nullified if the Pythagorean theorem were discarded, which would lead to the collapse of trigonometry as a whole. The collapse of the Pythagorean theorem would also undermine the credibility of functions for circles, ellipses, and so forth.

Trigonometry Has No Functions

The smallest measurement of an angle is a second. One degree is equal to sixty minutes, and one minute consists of sixty seconds. There is gap between every second. For instance, there is a gap between 67°48'22" and 67°48'23". If we plotted a sine Θ versus Θ graph, we would not be able to link all the dots with a curve on the graph paper because the smallest measurement of an angle is a second and there is a gap between every second. In other words, the gap between every second is undefined. Therefore, we could never link those dots with a curve.

Since the dimensions of the adjacent leg, opposite leg, and hypotenuse for all right-angled triangles are unique, they are not associated with each other as dictated by the Pythagorean theorem. Therefore, even if we link all the dots together with a curve, we shouldn't expect it to be a smooth curve, mainly because all right-angled triangles are unique.

According to trigonometry – which leads us to find that tangent Θ versus Θ graph has asymptotes when Θ is 90°, 270°, ... or –90°, –270°, ... – how can tangent Θ function if there are discontinuities at various asymptotes in a tangent Θ versus Θ graph? For instance, when Θ is 90°, the value of the tangent is $+\infty$ on the left side of the asymptote and $-\infty$ on the right side, which proves not only that tangent Θ discontinues at the asymptotes but also that the value of tangent Θ diverges to positive infinite on one side of an asymptote and to negative infinite on the other side. Moreover, at the points of the asymptotes, when Θ is 90°, tangent Θ is undefined. This strongly suggests that tangent Θ is not a function, mainly because tangent Θ versus Θ graph is made up of several discontinued curves – and a function is a continuous curve from negative infinite to positive infinite.

The value of sine Θ is the ratio of the opposite leg over the hypotenuse of a right-angled triangle with a corresponding angle of Θ. For every different value of Θ, its corresponding value of sine Θ is unique. If we draw several right-angled triangles of different sizes and all of these have the similar angle Θ, then the value of sine Θ for all these right-angled triangles is the same. In other words, all different sizes of right-angled triangles that have a similar angle Θ are proportional to each other. On the other hand, for every different right-angled triangle that has a distinct angle Θ, the trigonometry ratios must be distinct and unique.

The dimensions of the adjacent leg, opposite leg, and hypotenuse of a right-angled triangle are not strictly associated with each other as dictated by the Pythagorean theorem. This is parallel to our belief that the various trigonometric ratios of a right-angled triangle with a specific corresponding angle Θ are unique. Therefore, every different value of Θ corresponds with a unique trigonometry ratio as each is tabulated on the trigonometry table shown in most mathematic textbooks.

Since sine Θ versus Θ graph is made up of dots, it is not a function. Therefore, there exists no limit along the curve of a sine Θ versus Θ graph. Any increment that is smaller than a second (i.e. a degree) is undefined. This clearly shows that there exists no limit along the curve of the sine Θ versus Θ graph. The same applies to other trigonometry ratios such as cosine and tangent. All so-called trigonometric functions have no corresponding derivatives.

Let's call a spade a spade and say that a line is different from a right-angled triangle, as a line has no hypotenuse or opposite leg. Therefore, a horizontal or vertical line is a line; by no means is it a right-angled triangle. So, zero and ninety degrees must be excluded from the tabulated trigonometry table in most mathematics textbooks.

Ancient trigonometry was based on a very simple concept. A tabulated trigonometry table helped people figure out the specific dimension of a right-angled triangle that corresponded with a specific angle Θ if one of the dimensions of a right-angled triangle was known. In addition, the trigonometry table is based on raw diagrams of right-angled triangles with angles measuring from one degree to eighty-nine degrees. Furthermore, the value of sine Θ to its corresponding angle Θ is calculated by dividing the length of the triangle's corresponding opposite leg by the length of the hypotenuse. On the other hand, the value of cosine Θ is calculated by dividing the length of the adjacent leg by the length of the hypotenuse. The value of tangent Θ is derived by dividing the length of the opposite leg by the length of the adjacent leg.

Let's look at an example. Say that a carpenter wants to construct a wooden roof truss for a house that has a width of 10 metres. The carpenter finds out that the angle between the rafter and the horizontal beam of the truss is 30°. What are the measurements for the height of the truss and the length of the rafter? The length of the adjacent truss is 5 metres. Based on the trigonometry table, the values of cosine 30° and tangent 30° are 0.8660 and 0.5774 respectively. Keep in mind that cosine Θ is the ratio of the adjacent leg over the hypotenuse, and tangent Θ is the ratio of the opposite leg over the adjacent leg. The measurement of the rafter's hypotenuse may be obtained by dividing the base of the truss, 5 metres, by cosine 30°, or 0.8660, for a quotient of 5.7737 metres. On the other hand, the height of the truss is equal to the width of the truss: 5 metres. If we multiply this by tangent 30°, we get 2.887 metres. This example shows the simple application of trigonometry in ancient times. Unfortunately, at the turn of the sixteenth century, some smart mathematicians like François Viète, Thomas Finck, and Johannes Werner turned trigonometry into a perplexing and complex philosophy that defied the sanctity and logic of mathematics. These mathematicians believed that trigonometry consisted of functions. Undoubtedly, they were all *wrong*! They didn't comprehend the development of trigonometry from its inception. No trigonometry entities are functions (i.e. there is always a gap in between every increment of a second, and any increment that is smaller than a second is considered to be undefined. Therefore, a curve can't link up all those dots. Thus, those alleged trigonometric functions actually turn out not to be functions), and the hypotenuse, adjacent leg, and opposite leg of a right-angled triangle are not associated as dictated by the Pythagorean theorem.

The Law of Sine

In this segment, we will determine whether or not the angle of an obtuse triangle, which is greater than 90° but less than 180°, has a unique sine. Angles α and β are the respective inner angles of the right-angled triangles EAC and EBC, as shown in Figure 11. Furthermore, γ angle is the inner angle of the right-angled triangle BCH. Subsequently, the length of the opposite leg of right-angled triangles EBC, EAC, and BCH are quantified, as shown in Figure 11.\

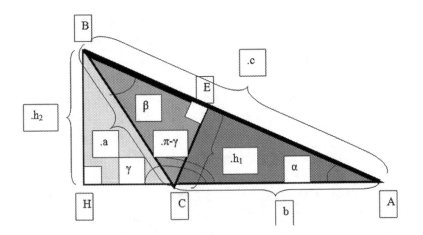

We perform the following calculation to find the length of h_1 based on the right-angled triangle *EAC*:

$$\sin \alpha = h_1/b \text{ or } h_1 = b \sin \alpha \qquad \rightarrow \qquad \text{Equation 1}$$

We perform the following calculation to find the length of h_1 based on the right-angled triangle *EBC*:

$$\sin \beta = h_1/a \text{ or } h_1 = a \sin \beta \qquad \rightarrow \qquad \text{Equation 2}$$

We combine equation 1 and equation 2, as shown below:

$$h1 = b \sin \alpha = a \sin \beta$$

$$\rightarrow \qquad (\sin \alpha)/a = (\sin \beta)/b$$

We perform the following calculation to find the length of h_2 based on the right-angled triangle *BAH*:

$$\sin \alpha = h_2/c \text{ or } h_2 = c \sin \alpha \qquad \rightarrow \qquad \text{Equation 3}$$

We perform the following calculation to find the length of h_2 based on the right-angled triangle *BCH*:

$$\sin \gamma = h_2/a \text{ or } h_2 = a \sin \gamma \qquad \rightarrow \qquad \text{Equation 4}$$

We combine equation 3 and equation 4, as shown below:

$$h_2 = c \sin \alpha = a \sin \gamma$$

$$\rightarrow \qquad (\sin \alpha)/a = (\sin \gamma)/c$$

None of the foregoing equations involve angle $(\pi - \gamma)$. In other words, none of those equations have anything to do with angle $(\pi - \gamma)$. Unfortunately, some smart-alec mathematicians believe that $\sin \gamma$ is equal to $\sin (\pi - \gamma)$, as shown below.

$$\sin \gamma = \sin (\pi - \gamma) = h_2/a$$

There is no proof that sin γ is equal to sin $(\pi - \gamma)$, as none of the foregoing equations have anything to do with angle $(\pi - \gamma)$. The angles involved in deriving those equations are angles β, α, and γ. There is no proof whatsoever for us to use for drawing the conclusion that sin γ is equal to sin $(\pi - \gamma)$. In reality, the range of trigonometry ratios is defined only for angles that are greater than zero but smaller than 90°. Again, lines, whether they are vertical or horizontal, are not right-angled triangles and therefore should be excluded from the trigonometry table. Any angles that are greater than 90° are considered to be undefined.

The Law of Cosine

In this section, the author will expose the fallacy that the value of the cosine ratio of an inner angle of an obtuse triangle will have a negative value as dictated by the law of cosine.

The law of cosine is based on the Pythagorean theorem. In reality, the Pythagorean theorem is used only to find an approximate length of the hypotenuse of a right-angled triangle. It is not true that the Pythagorean theorem is able to quantify the length of the hypotenuse of a right-angled triangle with accuracy. But this is not the only defect of the law of cosine. The lengths of the adjacent leg, opposite leg, and hypotenuse of a right-angled triangle are all supposed to be positive in dimension, regardless if any one of them has a negative value, such as the portion that is in a specific quadrant, especially when the Pythagorean theorem is to be utilized in the computation. In other words, the dimensions for the adjacent leg, opposite leg, and hypotenuse of a right-angled triangle must be positive in value when the Pythagorean theorem is used in the computation, regardless if a portion of the adjacent leg of the right-angled triangle is negative in value. The Pythagorean theorem was derived based on a 3-4-5 right-angled triangle, where the lengths of the adjacent leg, opposite leg, and hypotenuse are all positive dimensions. But when mathematicians developed the law of cosine, they unfortunately validated the idea that a portion of the adjacent leg can be negative in value.

The proof for justifying the derivation of the correct law of cosine is based on Figure 12.

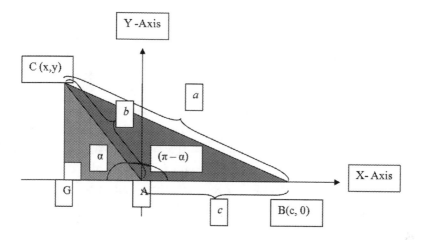

Obtuse triangle *CAB* has an inner angle of $(\pi - \alpha)$. The dimensions of the obtuse triangle *CAB* are *a*, *b*, and *c*, as shown in Figure 12. Then, we employ the Pythagorean theorem to quantify the length of the hypotenuse of the right-angled triangle *CBG*.

The length of the opposite leg of the right-angled triangle *CAG* is $(\sin \alpha)b$. On the other hand, the length of the adjacent leg of the right-angled triangle *CBG* is $(c + b \cos \alpha)$. Of course, the length of the hypotenuse of the right-angled triangle *CBG* is *a*. We utilize the Pythagorean theorem to quantify the length of the hypotenuse, *a* in terms of *b*, *c*, and α, as shown in the following equation:

$$a^2 = b^2 (\sin^2\alpha) + (c + b \cos \alpha)^2$$
$$\rightarrow \quad a^2 = b^2 \sin^2 \alpha + c^2 + b^2 \cos^2 \alpha + 2 b c \cos \alpha$$
$$\rightarrow \quad a^2 = b^2 (\sin^2 \alpha + \cos^2 \alpha) + c^2 + 2 b c \cos \alpha$$

Since $\sin^2 \alpha + \cos^2 \alpha = 1$, we get the following equation:

$$\rightarrow \quad a^2 = b^2 + c^2 + 2b c \cos \alpha$$

The correct formula for quantifying the hypotenuse of an obtuse triangle is $a^2 = b^2 + c^2 + 2b c$ cosine α, as shown above. On the other hand, the correct equation that we have derived is clearly different from the original formula of the law of cosine, as shown below:

$$a^2 = b^2 + c^2 - 2 b c \cos \alpha$$

The term $-2\,b\,c\cos\alpha$ is supposed to be $+2\,b\,c\cos\alpha$. This proves that the original law of cosine is wrong. Regardless of which quadrant a portion of a dimension of a right-angled triangle is in, all dimensions for the adjacent leg, opposite leg, and hypotenuse must be positive in value, especially when the Pythagorean theorem has been used in the computation.

In addition, angle $(\pi - \alpha)$ is not employed in deriving the equation of the law of cosine. Of course, this example of the derivation of the law of cosine does not imply in any way that cosine $(\pi - \alpha)$ is equal to cosine α. The error in deriving the law of cosine is in validating a portion of the adjacent leg as being negative in value, leading to the misunderstanding that the value of cosine of the second quadrant has a negative value. In other words, the error also leads us to believe that only the value of cosine of the second quadrant has a positive value. In conclusion, the correct derivation of the law of cosine (i.e. $a^2 = b^2 + c^2 + 2b\,c\cos\alpha$) does not imply that the cosine in the second quadrant will have a negative value.

The errors in deriving the law of cosine (i.e. the Pythagorean theorem gives us only an approximate length for a hypotenuse. In addition, we must treat all dimensions of the triangle – the adjacent leg, the opposite leg, and the hypotenuse – as being positive in value even when a portion of one of those dimensions is negative in value because it is in negative quadrant, especially when the Pythagorean theorem has been used in the computation. Furthermore, the law of cosine presumes that cosine $(\pi - \alpha)$ is equal to cosine α without substantiating it with mathematical proof) leads us to believe that any trigonometric ratio of any inner angle of a right-angled triangle that is greater than zero but less than 90° will be well defined. In other words, any inner angle that is greater than 90° should be considered invalid. Hopefully this fallacy in the law of cosine will be rectified in the future.

Chapter 3

Vector

The Validity of Dot Product

The dot product is recognized as the scalar product of two vectors. The outcome of the scalar product is equal to the multiplication of the length of two different vectors and the inner angle Θ between those two vectors, as shown in Figure 13.

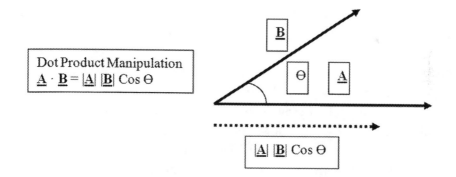

The dot product formula is derived based on the law of cosine. Since the law of cosine is defective, this implies that the dot product is a flawed mathematical concept. Dot product is commonly used to quantify the work done by force in displacing an object. For instance, $\mathbf{F} \cdot \mathbf{s}$ shows force ($\mathbf{F}$) and the dot product ($\mathbf{s}$), which equates to $|\mathbf{F}|\,|\mathbf{s}|$ cosine Θ, where $\mathbf{F}$ is an acting force and $\mathbf{s}$ is displacement. In other words, a component of force ($\mathbf{F}$) that is parallel to the direction of displacement does the *real* work, as $\mathbf{F} \cdot \mathbf{s}$ can be rewritten as $|\mathbf{F}|$ cos Θ $|\mathbf{s}|$. The outcome of the dot product (i.e. $|\mathbf{F}|$ cos Θ $|\mathbf{s}|$) is a scalar. We assume that a moving object is a point, as if the object were a dot. We also assume that the other component, force ($\mathbf{F}$), which is perpendicular to displacement $\mathbf{s}$, will do no work simply because the object is not displacing in that direction. This explanation sounds practical, but then again the surface of the earth is not entirely flat. The earth looks rather like an imperfect spheroid. Even a plain on the earth that appears to be completely flat turns out not to be flat at all. With this fact in mind, we discover that a small amount of work must be done by the perpendicular component of force ($\mathbf{F}$). Of course, the work done by the perpendicular component of force ($\mathbf{F}$) might be minimal, but it is not completely zero. In addition, the earth is not an ideal environment, as friction occurs whenever we try to move anything. In other words, frictional force always goes against anything that is in motion or trying to move. Undoubtedly, the normal force has some influence on the magnitude of the incurred friction; therefore, pushing and pulling on something will have different effects. Generally it is more effective to pull than to push an object. This strongly suggests that the formula to compute the work done on a moving object like $|\mathbf{F}|\,|\mathbf{s}|\cos\Theta$ may not be accurate because it does not take into consideration the presence of frictional force. The equation $|\mathbf{F}|\,|\mathbf{s}|\cos\Theta$ that computes the work done by an acting force that is displacing an object is too idealistic and simplistic. The application of dot product manipulation in the computation of the work done by force ($\mathbf{F}$) that is moving an object with a displacement of $\mathbf{s}$ is just a rough approximation of the work done by the force ($\mathbf{F}$). It sounds very simple to quantify the work done by force ($\mathbf{F}$) in displacing an object with displacement $\mathbf{s}$, but we are already bogged down miserably. It is difficult to know exactly how much work has been done by force $\mathbf{F}$ mainly because we do not know how much work has actually been done to overcome air resistance, for instance. Bear in mind that frictional force may not be a constant all the time simply because the surface of the platform is never homogenous. In other words, the frictional force is actually higher well before an object starts to move, and it actually gets smaller once an object is moving. In addition, it is very difficult to quantify the amount of force that is applied to an object since it is also extremely difficult to maintain a constant acting force. Even though we may carry out a simple experiment, it is simply impossible to quantify the work done by a force $\mathbf{F}$ with accuracy given the various uncertainties that we might encounter.

Some mathematicians and physicists believe that satellites can go round and round Planet Earth and never lose any significant amount of energy. According to these mathematicians and physicists, this is because moving satellites are constantly tangential to their orbits. Since cos 90° is equal to zero, they aver, satellites do no work when circling Planet Earth. This explanation seems plausible, but in reality the orbits of all satellites are not perfectly circular. They are elliptical. Therefore, satellites do not really move tangentially to their orbits all the time. This calls into question the validity of the dot product.

The reason that satellites do not seem to lose their energy despite their continuous circling of the earth is that their total energy seems to be conserved rather well. When satellites are moving closer to earth, their kinetic energy increases because some of the localized gravitational potential energy is converted to kinetic energy. In contrast, moving satellites that are farther away from earth experience a slowdown in speed as more of their kinetic energy transforms back into localized gravitational potential energy. This indirectly implies that the velocity of all satellites is never a constant, because the force that is acting on them is always varying. Generally, a satellite's total energy is conserved for quite some time; therefore, it can spin round and round the earth as if it is doing no work at all. But a satellite does lose some of its energy gradually as a result of interacting with sparse gaseous molecules within the upper atmosphere. Subsequently, the satellite's altitude decreases gradually. The satellites that are equipped with rocket propulsion can readjust the altitude of their orbit from time to time, whereas those without rocket propulsion eventually tailspin out of control before burning out in the upper thermosphere.

Assume the universe is a big spheroid which will continue to expand outwardly away from the centre of the universe as time progresses. Our solar system, a small dot within the universe, will also move gradually outwards in parallel with the expansion of the universe. As the solar system moves outwardly from the centre of the universe, the matter and objects within the solar system increase in universal gravitational potential energy and, at the same time, experience a reduction in kinetic energy. In real time, the moon and satellites will continue to orbit the earth and will preserve their kinetic energy in the short term. This is because only a negligible amount of kinetic energy is transformed into universal gravitational potential energy in parallel with the expansion of the universe. Undoubtedly, the earth itself is also experiencing significant slowdown. The duration of a single complete rotation of the earth is slowing down, but not to a significant degree. An atomic clock registered that the earth would take a longer time to complete a single revolution around the sun. This clearly supports the notion that any celestial objects that are moving outwards in parallel with the expansion of the universe will transform more and more of their kinetic energy into universal gravitational potential energy. Both transverse kinetic energy and rotational energy are affected by the expansion of the universe, but they most likely change at different rates. We know that the universe expands rather slowly in real time, but not because of the existence of so-called black bodies. This is simply because more and more of the kinetic energy of celestial objects converts to universal gravitational potential energy; therefore, the expansion rate of the universe naturally experiences slowdown as a result of the diminished kinetic energy of the celestial bodies. Those black bodies, if they exist anywhere within the universe, must have come into existence sometime after the Creation. Therefore, the existence of black bodies is not a plausible explanation for why the universe expanded at a much faster rate in the past but has experienced a slowdown recently. On the other hand, the conversion of more and more kinetic energy into universal gravitational potential energy easily explains the slowing down of the expansion of the universe in this current phase of expansion.

Most satellites also increase their content of matter (i.e. the number of stockpiled photons that they possess), as their capability for stockpiling photons improves as a result of the increase in their universal gravitational potential energy. When the altitude of a satellite changes, the satellite's number of photons becomes subject to change as well. This enables us to comprehend how crystallized water molecules within a cloud have a different stockpile of stationary photons that makes them different from ordinary water molecules at sea level. An increase in localized gravitational potential energy at a higher altitude allows the crystallized water molecules to amass more stationary photons. The air molecules trapped within the ice crystals of a dense cloud can easily be ionized when gusts of wind brush against them. Subsequently, those stationary electrons drift farther away from their nuclei; therefore, the transfer of electrons can take place rather easily among fast-moving air molecules that become trapped within a dense cloud because of the presence of a gusty wind. The natural phenomenon of lightning strongly suggests to us that a cloud becomes ionized rather easily when it experiences an increase in localized gravitational potential energy at a higher altitude. Normally, traces of nitric acid and carbonic acid are found in rainwater (undoubtedly the industrial emissions from factories contribute to the formation of nitric and carbonic acids in rainwater. But the presence of nitric and carbonic acids in rainwater in the middle of a desert, for instance, clearly suggests that both acids were formed amid the presence of lightning). This indirectly supports the notion that air molecules, such as nitrogen and carbon dioxide molecules trapped within a cloud, react with other air molecules, especially oxygen molecules, during a lightning storm to form nitric and carbonic acids before they dissolve in precipitation. This also suggests that water molecules at sea level are actually somewhat stable and resistant to ionization. By providing the explanation of the lightning phenomenon, the author hopes to reinforce the belief that satellites, which revolve around the earth at high altitudes, are able to accumulate a sizeable number of stationary photons.

Scientists reckon that the universe is currently expanding at a slower pace. Our solar system, which is on the edge of the Milky Way, is believed to be drifting outwardly away from the centre of the universe in parallel with the expansion of the universe. Planet Earth is subjected to radiation from the sun every day, yet it experiences no dramatic rise in temperature. This clearly suggests that as the earth increases its universal gravitational potential energy, it has a greater "appetite" for stationary photons. Therefore, it is not surprising that a deserted land on a moonless night fills with complete darkness. Aided by atomic clocks, scientists have managed to prove that the earth takes slightly longer than a fraction of a second to make a complete revolution around the sun. There are two reasons that the earth is slowing down. One reason is that more of the earth's kinetic energy is being converted to universal gravitational potential energy, which causes the earth to slow down. The other reason is that the earth is becoming more massive and, as a result, has an increased capacity to mop up more and more photons from its surroundings, especially the sun. The more massive the earth becomes, the more it slows down. The same effect applies to satellites that are revolving around the earth. These satellites also collect more and more stationary photons from their surroundings; therefore, their kinetic energy decreases gradually as some of that kinetic energy is used to mobilize the additional mass gained by the satellites. Also, some of that kinetic energy is gradually transformed into universal gravitational potential energy. Most satellites don't seem to experience such a dramatic loss of kinetic energy. Therefore, the author agrees that it must be the interaction between the satellite's molecules and the molecules of the upper atmosphere that decreases a satellite's kinetic energy at a much faster rate than the expansion of the universe does. Then again, there doesn't seem to be a reliable timepiece for measuring this, as even an atomic clock is not immune from the effects of the expansion of the universe. This is because the kinetic energy of atoms and molecules alike will experience slowdown gradually as a result of the expansion of the universe. More and more kinetic energy will be transformed into universal gravitational potential energy. For instance, the duration of a second as measured by an atomic clock today may not be the same as the duration of a second as measured by an atomic clock a century in the future. Most important of all is the effect of the expansion of the universe on the life span of humankind. Excluding the benefits of better healthcare, if human beings experience longevity as a direct result of the expansion of the universe, then we will perceive time as having moved more slowly than before. In addition, the perception of time is subjective, especially in the absence of a truly reliable timepiece.

In conclusion, satellites can remain in rotation around the earth for a long duration mainly because their total amount of energy is very well conserved. Dot product fails to explain the reason why satellites continue circling the earth for quite a long duration as if they are doing no work. This clearly proves that dot product is a flawed mathematical concept.

The Definition of Cross Product

The cross product is commonly used to quantify torque motion. The mathematical expression of vector **a** and cross vector **b**, **a** × **b**, equals $|a|\,|b|\sin\Theta\,\eta$. When the tails of two vectors are joined together, as shown in Figure 14, the magnitude of torque equals $|a|\,|b|\sin\Theta$. The vector η is a normal vector to the plane of both vector **a** and vector **b**. Furthermore, vector η signifies the axis of torque motion. The angle Θ is the angle between vector **a** and vector **b**. In addition, the right-hand rule is used to define the direction in which vector η is pointing to supplement the definition of cross product. When two vectors are parallel, their vector cross product is zero. Of course, the product of **a** × **b** is also zero if either vector **a** or **b** is zero.

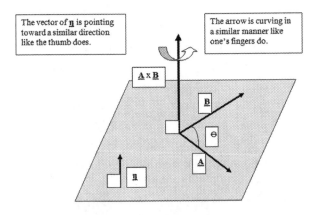

The vector of η is pointing toward a similar direction like the thumb does.

The arrow is curving in a similar manner like one's fingers do.

A×B

B

θ

A

η

If two vectors, such as forces, are acting on a similar point, they can be replaced by a net force only if that net force is acting on the same point. No torque is produced by the net force that is acting on a pivot, provided that the net force is acting on a moment arm. A moment arm is not a vector. Furthermore, a force that acts on a point on a moment arm does not move along that moment arm. In other words, such a moment arm is not qualified to be classified as a vector. Generally, torque exists because a force is acting on a moment arm, and the angle at which the force is acting on the moment arm is maintained despite the fact that the moment arm is spinning around. Similarly, a force or a couple of forces that are acting on a moment arm produce torque. The key is the moment arm. Of course, a point on the moment arm must be a pivot point, one that allows the moment arm to spin around.

According to the right-hand rule, $\mathbf{a} \times \mathbf{b}$ is different from $\mathbf{b} \times \mathbf{a}$. Shouldn't the direction of an acting force on a moment arm and the orientation of the plane in which the moment arm is freely rotating on a pivot determine the rotational direction of torque? The right-hand rule is not necessarily correct in determining the direction of the torque. It is also possible that the direction of torque as predicted by the right-hand rule contradicts the actual rotational direction of the torque.

Torque is a moment arm that is moving round and round on a pivot when a force/forces is/are acting on the moment arm. Therefore, a spinning motion has no well-defined direction. It is difficult to determine whether or not to classify torque as a vector. On second thought, torque without a well-defined direction should not be classified as a vector. This is because a vector must have a well-defined direction and magnitude, neither of which torque possesses. Therefore, the outcome of a cross product should be a scalar.

Attempting to explain torque by introducing a normal vector, η, to symbolize torque only leads to confusion. There is no creation of a new force that is acting perpendicular to the plane of the torque as a result of the torque itself. If there were a newly created force in existence that is acting perpendicular to the plane of the torque, then the torque's plane would drift in the direction as dictated by that newly created normal force. Undoubtedly, the plane of the torque would remain static, which strongly suggests that there is no existing a normal vector η that is acting against the plane of torque. Indirectly, this implies that the mathematical concept of cross product does not align with reality.

In addition, the cross product dictates that the direction of torque depends on which vector has crossed another vector first (rather than depending on the direction of an acting force that is acting on a moment arm) and also on the plane where a moment arm freely rotates at a pivot. The so-called right-hand rule is completely confusing. It doesn't take into account which vector is crossed with another vector to determine the direction of torque. Isn't it that the movement plane of a moment arm hinges on the design of the moment arm itself, as well as on the direction of a force that is acting on the moment arm?

In reality, the plane of torque remains stationary at a pivot point around which its moment arm continues to rotate. In conclusion, the improper manner in which the cross product has been defined clearly undermines the validity and usefulness of the cross product.

Triple Scalar Products

The triple scalar product of three vectors, such as **a**, **b**, and **c**, is vector **a** dot product with the result of vector **b** crossing vector **c**, in which the outcome of the triple product is found to be scalar, as shown below.

$$[\mathbf{a}, \mathbf{b}, \mathbf{c}] = \mathbf{a} \cdot (\mathbf{b} \times \mathbf{c})$$

Modern mathematicians believe that the triple scalar product has a geometric interpretation, which is shown in Figure 15; in addition, mathematicians presume that the volume of a parallelogram with co-terminal edges **a**, **b**, and **c** represents the outcome of mathematical manipulation of the triple scalar product of [**a**, **b**, **c**] as **a** · (**b** × **c**).

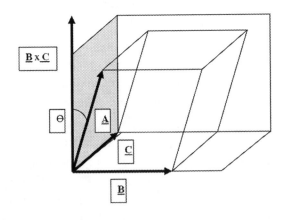

Assuming that the cross product operation is valid, vector **b**'s cross product with moment arm **c** is equal to a moment, which is a scalar. This is mainly because torque has no well-defined direction. Because of this, the outcome of a cross product is not a vector. The dot product of force **a** with torque (i.e. a scalar) that is rotating round and round on its pivot is an invalid mathematical operation because it is impossible for torque to form a triangle whose angles can be measured before the magnitude of the dot product between vector **a** and the moment arm of (**b** × **c**) is quantified. It is impossible for vector **a** to act on the moment arm. Vector **a** can most likely act on the pivot of the moment arm. Obviously vector **a** does not have any bearing on the torque if it is acting on the pivot on which the moment arm is hingeing. If the pivot of a moment arm were ever set in motion by the acting vector **a**, then the pivot would likely drift in the direction dictated by the acting vector **a**. In other words, the direction of movement of a pivot and of vector **a** is always parallel; therefore, the employment of dot product is unnecessary.

On the other hand, **a** · (**b** × **c**) indirectly implies that vector **a** is acting against torque; as a result, the torque is moving in the direction of the torque, as vector **a** is the dot product of (**b** × **c**). But torque (**b** × **c**) has no well-defined direction since it is torque. In conclusion, the triple scalar product makes no sense as a mathematical operation. Therefore, it is naïve for a person to believe that the triple scalar product has any geometrical interpretation.

Invalidation of the Divergence Concept

The author stresses that any mathematical expression must obey the law of conservation of energy and the law of conservation of matter. By the same token, any mathematical expression must reflect reality – an occurrence of natural phenomenon – if it is to be considered valid. Many mathematical expressions and definitions, including the definition of divergence, should be formulated based on modelling through experimentation. If an experiment is designed to be as simple as possible, then data can be collected easily and observations can be recorded without ambiguity. Most experiments in fluid mechanics should be carried out under a steady-state environment to facilitate data collection and enhance observation.

The volume of space is represented by a cube, as shown in Figure 16. The x-axis, y-axis, and z-axis are used to denote the three-dimensional physicality of the cube. There are three steady-state flows in different directions that are parallel to the x-axis, y-axis, and z-axis of a cube, as shown in Figure 16. This diagram is important because it shows the methodology used for defining the divergence.

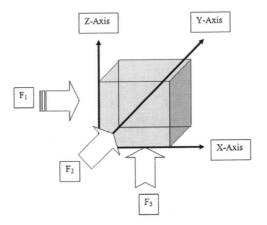

Before the author judges the validity of the definition of divergence, let's take a look at the contemporary definition of divergence as indicated below:

The divergence of vector field $\underline{F} = F_1 \underline{i} + F_2 \mathrm{j} + F_3 \underline{k}$ is a scalar field, denoted by div $\underline{F}$, which is defined by div $\underline{F} = \partial F_1/\partial x + \partial F_2/\partial y + \partial F_3/\partial z$.

The steady-state flow implies that a certain volume of fluid flows into the volume of the cube from one specific boundary of that cube and then passes through the cube before flowing out of the opposite boundary of the cube. A steady-state flow is a directional flow. All volumetric flow of F_1, F_2, and F_3 will flow through said cube parallel to the x-axis, y-axis, and z-axis respectively.

In reality, turbulence occurs when the volumetric flow of F_1, F_2, and F_3 spurts within the cube and intermingles, which disrupts the smooth flow of fluid into and out of the cube. Frictional losses then take place within the cube. The volume of the flow of F_1, F_2, and F_3 out of the cube from their respective opposite sides may not be a perfect steady-state flow because the existence of turbulence and friction prevents the fluid from compressing.

We heavily rely on simple mathematical modelling when trying to understand a complex environment or phenomenon. More often than not, simple mathematical modelling fails miserably in describing complex natural phenomena. Similarly, no mathematical equation or mathematical model is 100 per cent accurate when describing any natural phenomenon. We often fall into the trap of believing that there is a specific mathematical equation to accurately describe every natural phenomenon. In reality, humankind's ability to understand nature is limited to a certain extent because our ability to visualize is limited. Therefore, we often simplify complex problems by applying simple mathematical equations to them. Usually the modelling we do does not do a good job of describing the actual natural phenomenon. Moreover, our understanding of natural phenomena is limited because we fail to visualize what takes place at the microscopic level (i.e. atomic level) or because the set-up is too complex and complicated (i.e. turbulence is present, frictional losses are experienced, or viscosity changes because of a variation in temperature).

Lastly, with regard to the divergence concept, it fails to examine the real behaviour of fluid that flows into an imaginary cube mainly because the concept is too simple. It fails to account for the effect of turbulence and frictional losses, which might disrupt the free flow of fluid into a chamber and which may cause the flow out from the opposite direction to occur in something other than a steady state. Also, the volume of liquid that flows in and out from the same axis might not be exactly the same. Of course, the total volume of fluid that flows into and out of the imaginary cube might or might not be the same under a steady-state condition depending on the fluid's characteristics.

Chapter 4

Calculus

Trigonometric "Functions" Have No Derivatives

There is no obvious relationship among the adjacent leg, opposite leg, and hypotenuse of any right-angled triangle since the Pythagorean theorem provides only an approximate length of the hypotenuse. Therefore, every right-angled triangle is unique, and each right-angled triangle's ratios of sine, cosine, tangent, etc., are unique. The smallest measurement of an angle is one second. Thus, any angle that is between two consecutive seconds is considered to be undefined. These two factors indicate to us that so-called trigonometric functions are actually not functions. It is forbidden to link all the dots on a sine-versus-angles graph, for instance, simply because the gaps between the dots are undefined.

One second is equal to $1°/3600$ or $0.0002778°$. If $\Delta\Theta$ converges on something that is smaller than $0.0002778°$, there will be no limit because the angle in between each second is undefined. Undoubtedly, the trigonometric ratios of any right-angled triangle are unique. This implies that the value of sine, for instance, does not guarantee a smooth transition for different successive right-angled triangles with increments smaller than one second since they are undefined. In conclusion, there are no limits for so-called trigonometric functions because they aren't functions. Since no limit exists for any trigonometric function, none of the so-called trigonometric functions have corresponding derivatives.

The Family of 1/x Functions Are Invalid

Since ancient times, mathematicians have believed that they could integrate all functions that make up the family of 1/x functions except for the function of 1/x itself. Because of this, they are adamant in believing that the function 1/x must have an anti-derivative. After realizing that it was impossible to integrate the function 1/x, mathematicians introduced a completely new function, ln(x), as an anti-derivative of function 1/x. The function ln(x) is equal to $\log_e x$, where the logarithm of the base e is called a natural logarithm. On the other hand, 2.718 is approximate to e. Since e is an irrational number, this indirectly means that the natural logarithm may be a flawed concept. Undoubtedly, ln(x) is defined as the anti-derivative when x is larger than zero. In other words, ln(x) is undefined when x is zero or less than zero (i.e. when x has a negative value). If ln(x) is the anti-derivative of function 1/x, then it should able to quantify the area beneath the curve, regardless of whether the value of x is positive or negative. If an anti-derivative of a function is only valid within a certain range, as is the case with ln(x), then its validity is suspect. In other words, if the supposed anti-derivative of a function is valid only for a specific range of x and is undefined for other portions of x, then it is likely that the so-called anti-derivative is not the function's anti-derivative at all.

The so-called function 1/x is not a function. Assume that the unit of x is metre. In such a case, the unit of the function 1/x would be 1/m. This has no specific meaning (i.e. it makes no sense in the physical world) and does not exist in reality. The so-called function 1/x actually turns out not to be a function; therefore, it should not have an anti-derivative. Even though the function 1/x^2 seems like an anti-derivative, it is not a function either, because 1/m^2 is meaningless (as it presumes that the unit for x is metre). Another thing that proves that the family of functions including 1/x, 1/x^2, and so forth are not functions is that there is an asymptote at $x = 0$ or at the y-axis. The limit of $x = 0$ for the family of 1/x functions is undefined (for instance, 1/x^2 is undefined when x is zero). What is even more absurd about the function 1/x is that its limit is equal to $+\infty$ when x is at the positive of value zero (+0). On the other hand, its limit is $-\infty$ when x is at the negative side of zero (–0).

It is impossible to quantify the area beneath the curve of 1/x^3 at the place where the value of x is zero. Let's say that we want to integrate the place where x is equal to a and the place where x is equal to b, with both a and b being positive values. In other words, the area beneath the curve of function 1/x^3 from a to

b is the area in between the curve and the x-axis where the value of x is equal to negative infinite until b minus the area beneath the curve, where the value of x is equal to negative infinite until a. Since it is impossible to find the area beneath the curve of the function $1/x^3$ at the y-axis, the process for determining the area beneath the curve of function $1/x^3$, where the value of x is equal to $a-b$, is inconclusive. The logic is that it is impossible to quantify the area underneath the curve, especially when x is equal to zero. This deadlock will likely lead us to fail in our attempt to quantify the area beneath the function $1/x^3$ from where x is equal to $a-b$, with both a and b being positive numbers.

Ironically, it seems to be true that we are able to integrate the area beneath a curve of the function $1/x^3$ from a to b, with both a and b being positive numbers. And the quantified area beneath the curve turns out to be positive in value. In other words, most mathematicians would argue that one *is able* compute the area beneath a curve of function $1/x^3$ and that the answer seems to make sense. Since it is impossible to find the area beneath the curve when x is equal to zero, it is not clear how such a thing is possible! Why does it seem that the area underneath the curve for function $1/x^3$ between a and b is able to be computed? This is impossible! The answer that we obtain by integrating a function of $1/x^3$ from a to b, which is the area beneath a curve of the function $1/x^3$, is backwards! Actually we know that when x is positive infinite, the curve of the family of $1/x$ functions is presumed to be zero (i.e. the value of x can stretch to infinity, yet the value of $1/x^3$ is never equal to zero). Basically that is how the equation is defined in this case. In other words, we integrate the area underneath the curve of the family of $1/x$ functions, which breaks all the fundamental rules of calculus, as we are integrating in the direction indicated by the red arrow in Figure 17. So when x is equal to b, the anti-derivative of any of the functions belonging to the family of $1/x$ functions – except the function of $1/x$ – is the area underneath the curve that stretches from where x is positive infinite all the way to the dotted line in Figure 17, where x is equal to b. Similarly, the integration of the family of $1/x$ functions when x is equal to a indicates the area beneath a curve of the functions that also stretches from where x is positive infinite all the way until it reaches the dark green dotted line, where x is equal to a. Therefore, the area beneath a curve of the family of $1/x$ functions from where x is a to where x is b extends from positive infinite right up to the dark green dotted line of a minus the area underneath the curve from positive infinite until the red dotted line of b.

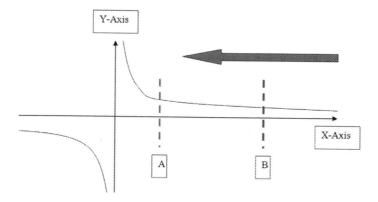

During a normal integration process, the equation always includes the area underneath a curve of *b* minus the area underneath a curve of *a*, with *b* being greater than *a*. But when integrating a family of 1/*x* functions, the equation is the other way around (i.e. the area underneath a curve from positive infinite to *a* minus the area underneath a curve from positive infinite right up to *b*, with *b* being greater than *a*). It is *possible* to carry out the integration of a family of 1/*x* functions assuming that a negative (i.e. a number preceded by a minus sign) multiplied by another negative transforms the number to positive (i.e. with a plus sign). Such a mathematical operation violates mathematical logic, as discussed in Chapter 1. Assume for the sake of illustration that a negative number multiplied by another negative number and resulting in a positive number is correct. This shows that the integration process of a function of $1/x^3$ from *a* to *b*, where both *a* and *b* are positive numbers and *b* is greater than *a*, is possible. Otherwise, the integration of a $1/x^2$ function is inoperable.

Since the methodology for quantifying the area underneath a curve of a family of 1/*x* functions defies all the basic rules of calculus, we should invalidate it. There are various convincing reasons for this. The first reason is that the so-called family of 1/*x* functions consists of no functions because the unit is absurd (i.e. the unit does not reflect the physical world; therefore, it cannot be a function. For instance, the unit of a function of 1/*x* is 1/metre, which makes no sense in the physical world). The second reason is that it is impossible to follow conventional calculus principles when integrating the area underneath a curve of any of the family of 1/*x* functions from negative infinite right to a certain positive point, for instance, simply because there is an asymptote when *x* is equal to zero and where *y* is undefined. Therefore it is impossible to quantify the area underneath the curve at the y-axis. The third reason for nullifying the integration of the family of $1/x$ functions is simply that the area underneath the curve integrates the other way around rather than strictly following the preset conventional calculus methodology.

A function is a continuous curve within a range of independent variables from $-\infty$ to $+\infty$. Furthermore, a function must comply with the physical world. It must exist in reality (i.e. its units must make sense when reflecting the physical world). The existence of an asymptote at the y-axis proves that there is discontinuity within the middle segment of a curve of the function. Therefore, the family of functions including $1/x$, $1/x^2$, and so forth don't have equivalent anti-derivatives simply because they are not functions.

Numerical Integration

Many mathematicians believe that there is a large number of continuous functions that have anti-derivatives that cannot be expressed as functions. Therefore, the fundamental theorem of calculus for evaluating a definite integral fails miserably[1] because it approximates as many decimal places as are deemed necessary. The trapezoidal rule and Simpson's rule are two of the many important foundations of modern numerical integration.

The definitions of the trapezoidal rule and Simpson's rule are expressed as mathematical equations, as shown below.

The Trapezoidal Rule

- b

$\int f(x)\, dx \approx$ sum of the areas of the trapezoids

- a

$$= \tfrac{1}{2}\, \Delta x\, [f(x_0) + f(x_1)] + \tfrac{1}{2}\, \Delta x\, [f(x_1) + f(x_2)] + \dots$$
$$+ \tfrac{1}{2}\, \Delta x\, [f(x_{n-2}) + f(x_{n-1})] + \tfrac{1}{2}\, \Delta x\, [f(x_{n-1}) + f(x_n)]$$
$$= \tfrac{1}{2}\, \Delta x\, [f(x_0) + 2 f(x_1) + 2 f(x_2) + \dots + 2 f(x_{n-1}) + f(x_n)]$$

Simpson's Rule

- b

$\int f(x)\, dx \approx$ sum of the areas bounded by a parabolic curve passing through points

- a

of $[x_i, f(x_i)]$, $[(x_{i+1}), f(x_{i+1})]$, and so forth

1   Grossman, Stanley I. *Calculus*. New York: Academic Press, 1981.

$$= a_2 + a_4 + a_6 + \ldots \ldots + a_{2n}$$

$$= \tfrac{1}{3} \Delta x \, [f(x_0) + f(x_1)] + \tfrac{1}{3} \Delta x \, [f(x_1) + f(x_2)] + \ldots$$
$$+ \tfrac{1}{3} \Delta x \, [f(x_{n-2}) + f(x_{n-1})] + \tfrac{1}{3} \Delta x \, [f(x_{n-1}) + f(x_n)]$$

$$= \tfrac{1}{3} \Delta x \, [f(x_0) + 4 f(x_1) + 2 f(x_2) + 4 f(x_3) + 2 f(x_4) + \ldots$$
$$+ 2 f(x_{2n-2}) + 4 f(x_{2n-1}) + f(x_{2n})]$$

The n in both the trapezoidal rule and Simpson's rule refers to the number of subintervals when evaluating the area beneath a curve. There are exactly as many n subintervals in both methods for quantifying the area underneath a curve of a function, but surprisingly many people believe that Simpson's rule provides a more accurate result than the trapezoidal rule provides. It is not true that there are twice as many subintervals when one is utilizing Simpson's rule as compared to the trapezoidal rule, as is commonly believed. It is not true that an answer obtained by using Simpson's rule to quantify the area underneath a curve will turn out to be more accurate than an answer arrived at by using the trapezoidal rule. As a matter of fact, it is the shape of the curve of a function that matters. For instance, if the curve of a function resembles a trapezoid without crests or a trough, then definitely the trapezoidal rule will be more accurate than Simpson's rule in quantifying the area beneath the curve.

To enhance the accuracy of the computation of an area underneath a curve by using numerical methods, one need not be restricted by employing only one method at a time. Employing both Simpson's rule and the trapezoidal rule definitely enhances the accuracy of the answer when quantifying the area underneath a curve of a function. According to the author, equally sized subintervals would greatly hinder the accuracy of the computation. The width and the number of subintervals at a particular point along a curve of a function depend entirely on the complexity of the geometrical shape of the curve rather than being predetermined with a prefixed width for the subintervals. Simpson's rule may be employed for the crests or troughs of a curve of a function to enhance the accuracy in computing the area underneath the curve of the function. On the other hand, the trapezoidal rule should be used for quantifying the region of the linear curve of the function to improve the accuracy of the computation. In any mathematical situation, flexibility and a better approach for resolving a problem undoubtedly lead one to a more accurate outcome.

The mathematical expressions for estimating the errors when utilizing either Simpson's rule or the trapezoidal rule to quantify the area underneath a curve are somewhat absurd. This is mainly because the widths of subintervals, which are predetermined without any examination of their ability to match the geometrical shape of a curve of a function, fail to quantify the area underneath the curve with accuracy, whether one employs the trapezoidal rule or Simpson's rule. Furthermore, not knowing the true answer of a computation in the first place makes it impossible to justify the incurred errors in said computation. But all efforts to reduce errors and make sufficient room for improving the accuracy of a computation will surely eliminate any unnecessary errors. This will ensure that we get closer to the true answer.

The Centroid of a Plane Region

The centroid of a plane region is also indirectly referred to as the centre of gravity. The centre of gravity is a special point, as the weight of an entire object is concentrated on it. The centre of gravity is normally located within a plane region, but sometimes a particular object's centre of gravity may be located outside the object itself.

To find the physical centroid of a right-angled triangle, draw a right-angled triangle on a piece of cardboard. Then use a pair of scissors to cut it out. Next, tie a string to one of its vertexes before hanging it. Tie the other end of the string to a stationary object. Let the right-angled triangle hang in the air. After a while, the right-angled triangle will become motionless and will sit at a tilt. When this happens, take a marker and mark the locus where the string passes through the right-angled triangle. Do the same thing for the other two vertexes. The centroid of this right-angled triangle is the intersection of the three lines passing through the right-angled triangle, as shown in Figure 18.

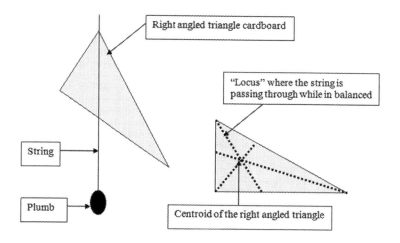

Most mathematicians believe that they can use the integration method to locate the centroid of a right-angled triangle without having to resort to a tedious routine like the one described above. Let's demonstrate how the integration method is used for finding the centroid of a right-angled triangle. The linear equation $-cx/a + c = y$, which cuts at $(0, c)$ on the y-axis and at $(a, 0)$ on the x-axis, forms a right-angled triangle, as shown in Figure 19.

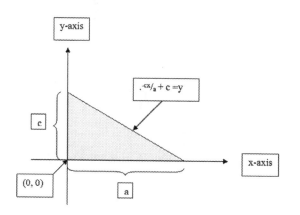

The definition of the centroid of a plane of an object is shown below:

$$\overline{x} = M_y/\mu = \rho \int_a^b x\,f(x)\,dx\,/\,\rho \int_a^b f(x)\,dx = \int_a^b x\,f(x)\,dx\,/\int_a^b f(x)\,dx$$

$$\bar{y} = M_x/\mu = {}^\rho/_2 \int_a^b [f(x)]^2 \, dx \,/\, \rho \int_a^b f(x) \, dx = \tfrac{1}{2} \int_a^b [f(x)]^2 \, dx \,/\, \int_a^b f(x) \, dx$$

Since the linear equation for $f(x)$ is ${}^{-cx}/_a + c = y$, to find the centroid we integrate from $x = 0$ to $x = a$, as shown below:

$$\bar{x} = \int_0^a \{-cx/a + c\} \times dx \,/\, \int_0^a \{-cx/a + c\} \, dx = \int_0^a \{-cx^2/a + cx\} \, dx \,/\, \int_0^a \{-cx/a + c\} \, dx$$

$$= -cx^3/3a + cx^2/2 \,\Big|_0^a\, /\, -cx^2/2a + cx \,\Big|_0^a\, = \{-ca^2/3 + ca^2/2\}/\{-ca/2 + ca\}$$

$$= \{ca^2/6\} \,/\, \{ca/2\} = a/3$$

$$\bar{y} = \tfrac{1}{2} \int_0^a \{-cx/a + c\}^2 \, dx \,/\, \int_0^a \{-cx/a + c\} \, dx$$

$$= \tfrac{1}{2} \int_0^a \{c^2x^2/a^2 + c^2 - 2c^2x/a\} \, dx \,/\, \int_0^a \{-cx/a + c\} \, dx$$

$$= \tfrac{1}{2} [c^2x^3/3a^2 + c^2 x - c^2x^2/a] \Big|_0^a \, /\, [-cx^2/2a + cx] \Big|_0^a$$

$$= \tfrac{1}{2} [c^2a^3/3a^2 + c^2a - c^2a^2/a] \,/\, [-ca^2/2a + ca] = \tfrac{1}{2} [c^2a/3] \,/\, [ca/2]$$

$$= {}^c/_3$$

The centroid of the right-angled triangle is $({}^a/_3, {}^c/_3)$. This implies, based on the outcome of the integration method, that the centroid of any right-angled triangle is one-third of its adjacent leg from the base of its right angle, as well as one-third of its height from the base of the triangle, as shown in Figure 20.

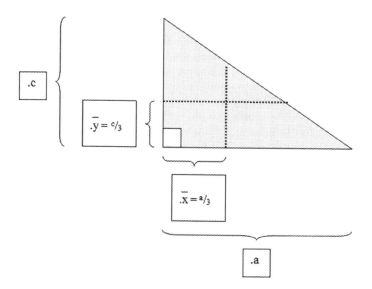

Modern mathematicians do not question the validity of the integration method when using it to determine the centroid of a right-angled triangle. In this section, the author tries to expose the error in using the integration method for finding the centroid of a right-angled triangle. Figure 21 shows the right-angled triangle ABC. Just assume that the centroid of $\triangle ABC$ is $^c/_3$ and $^a/_3$ based on the answer reached by using the method of integration.

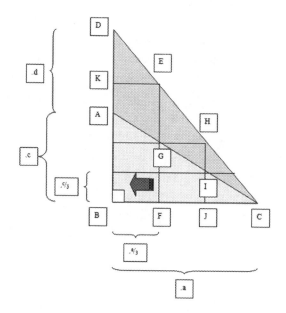

The right-angled triangle ABC is augmented to become ΔDBC, which is also a right-angled triangle. According to the integration method, the centroid of ΔDBC is ${}^{(d+c)}/_3$ and ${}^a/_3$, which indicate one-third of the triangle's height and width respectively. Our focus will be on the x-coordinate aspect of the centroid of ΔDBC, in which it is believed that the x-coordinate of the centre of gravity remains as ${}^a/_3$ since the width of ΔABC and ΔDBC both retain the same measurement. One important observation is that the area of the trapezoid $DEGA$ is always larger than the area of ΔECG. The length of BF and FC are ${}^a/_3$ and ${}^{2a}/_3$ respectively. Assume that the length of KA is equal to the length of HI. Then, the area of $\square KAGE$ is same as the area of $\square EGIH$. Since the length of DK is always longer than the length of HI, the area of ΔDKE must be larger than the area of ΔHIC. This strongly suggests that the centroid of the x-coordinate of ΔDBC may not remain as ${}^a/_3$. As a matter of fact, the x-coordinate centroid of ΔDBC will shift slightly towards the opposite side of ΔDBC, as shown by the arrow in Figure 22. This conclusively proves that the true x-coordinate centroid of the right-angled triangle DBC is not at ${}^a/_3$, as dictated by the integration method.

Similarly, the area of $\square \Delta GED$ must always be larger than the area of ΔGCE; therefore, the former's centroid y-coordinate will also shift upwards.

The x-coordinate centroid of augmented ΔDBC is not the same as that of ΔABC even though the two have a similar width. As a matter of fact, for ΔDBC, which is augmented from ΔABC, the centroid moves upwards and towards the opposite side of ΔDBC relative to the centroid of ΔABC. Since the method of integration fails to accurately determine the centroid of a right-angled triangle, naturally it fails to predict the centroid of the plane for any other geometrical shape except for a rectangular plane.

Given the drawbacks of the integration method in finding the centroid of a plane region, all design methodologies that reinforce the mechanics of materials need to be revamped. Otherwise, there is no easy way to find the centroid of a plane. In other words, a centroid of a plane region will have to be found by way of experimentation. Subsequently, the information should be tabulated in the form of a chart to facilitate the design process. The author believes that the safety of engineering design will be greatly enhanced after the error in the design process has been rectified.

The Truth of e^x Derivative

Modern mathematicians believe that e is an irrational number that is equal to 2.718281828459 … They also presume that e is a magic number, that the derivative of e^x remains as e^x.

Firstly, we examine the numerical function of e^x only as we scrutinize it before attaching a unit to it. Since e is an irrational number, there is no way to compute the exact value of e^x – simply because e has an infinite number of decimal places. In other words, the answer for the e^x computation is always indeterminate since e is an irrational number. Let's assume that the derivative of e^x is also e^x. If the computation is indeterminate, there is no way we can compare e^x and its derivate e^x. It is even more difficult to prove that they are exactly the same before we say that the derivative of e^x is also e^x without any ambiguity. Therefore, there is no convincing proof that the derivative of e^x is e^x. Furthermore, the function of e^x defies the law of conservation of matter and the law of conservation of energy, as either matter or energy, or both, can grow perpetually since e is an irrational number.

Let's assume that x has metre as a unit. When x has a value of 1.0038 metres, then $e^{1.0038m}$ has a unit, which makes no sense at all when compared to reality. In order to validate the function of e^x, let's express it again as (e apples)^x so that x is any real number without dimension or unit. This makes no sense either, because x has no accompanying unit. Even if (e apples)^x is valid, x is only valid if it is whole number. This is because the dimension of apples only makes sense when x is a whole number, but that would clearly restrict e^x as a function. In other words, the function of (e apples)^x is made up of dots only, which no curve is permitted to link up. Since (e apples)^x is not a function, (e apples)^x has no derivative or anti-derivative.

In conclusion, e is defined as an irrational number. This directly signals that something is amiss, as this definition violates the law of conservation of matter and the law of conservation of energy. When a unit is included with the function of e^x, this turns e^x into a non-function. Since e^x is not a function, it should have neither a derivative nor an anti-derivative.

Chapter 5

Statistics

Statistics – Past, Present, and Future

Statistics has become a crucial part of the world of quantum physics because it helps to describe the uncertain nature of the atomic world. Since the time that quantum mechanics emerged, the field of statistics has grown in importance (and keeps growing in importance). A few decades ago, statistics was developed into a complex philosophy for use in various new-found applications, such as descriptive statistics, statistical inference, probability theory, decision theory, and exploratory data analysis.

The advancement of quantum mechanics led to abuses in the application of statistics as the mathematical world laid out rules for dictating the behaviour of all creations of Almighty God. The convenience of statistical manipulation and its ability to distort the reality of collected data brought the field of statistics into opposition with reality. Any statistical manipulation that was intended to distort the distribution of collected data normally led to disillusion, fallacious conclusions, and a contradiction of reality. On the other hand, preserving statistics' accuracy when applying statistical manipulation in order to reflect reality enhances the usefulness of statistics.

The methodology of statistics helps in tabulating data, assessing distribution, determining the correlation among affected factors, and drawing conclusions when resolving complex problems. By the same token, statistics is a tool that helps us to define a correlation among the possible factors or influences that are the leading cause of a complex problem. For instance, we may use statistics to determine the correlation between smoking cigarettes and contracting lung cancer, comparing the number of smokers who eventually contract lung cancer to the entire population of smokers and non-smokers.

Besides smoking, some other factors may also encourage the development of lung cancer, such as one's stress level, lifestyle, living environment, and sleep patterns in addition to whether or not one overeats, overworks, gets physical exercise, consumes alcohol, is obese, and so forth. On top of this, other facets should be investigated, such as a person's genetic make-up, health consciousness or lack thereof, balanced diet or lack thereof, quality and amount of sleep, relationships (especially with a spouse), consumption of fish oil or lack thereof, consumption of specific mineral and vitamin supplements or lack thereof, and so forth, as these may affect the chance that a smoker will contract lung cancer. Simple research, such as seeking the correlation between cigarette smoking and lung cancer, can be influenced by many other possible factors, so the outcome of the research is not necessarily obvious.

Statistics retains its usefulness when it comes to transforming the perceived distribution based on collected data into an envisaged distribution. By the same token, distribution based on collected information is redistributed according to a person's perception, as the transformed distribution helps the intended user to justify his or her perceptions. Take for instance the grades for a test that are earned by of a group of physics students: A, B, C, D, and F. A fixed number of students will score A, B, C, D, or F after redistribution. No matter how easy the test is, some students will earn a failing grade after the scores are redistributed. In addition, the redistribution curve is always symmetrical in shape and the highest number of students earn an average grade.

Let's return to a topic explored in Chapter 1. As mentioned previously, American scientists in the 1980s proved that an electromagnetic wave consists of particles called photons. Electromagnetic waves are not waves after all; they are a cluster of dissipating photons per volume per time, and these clusters do not travel in waves. Chemical energy has so far been misunderstood, as it is derived from electrons whenever chemical reactions involve the sharing of electrons among reactants. The size of the orbital of both reactants and the ionic size of the products are different from one another before or after the chemical reaction. No doubt, stationary electrons either gain or lose the stationary photons that adhere to them. Surprisingly, a small quantity of heat, either released or absorbed during a chemical reaction, is derived from electrons. Quantum scientists overlook the importance of the nuclei of reactants in chemical reactions. They believe that the outer electrons of the reactants' atoms, which are the electrons involved in fostering chemical bonds, are often called valence electrons and that they appear where chemical energy is derived from the sharing of electrons. According to quantum scientists, a similarity in the configuration of the outer electrons (i.e. those that have the same number and type of valence electrons) is what makes the elements in a group resemble one another in their chemical behaviour. Quantum scientists do not wonder about what shape the valence electrons of a particular element take. We know that all protons are positively charged particles. On the other hand, neutrons are neutral. Except the hydrogen atom (with the added exceptions of deuterium and tritium), the nuclei of all other elements contain both protons and neutrons. Obviously, protons distance themselves from one another while they are inside a nucleus. Undoubtedly, protons and neutrons within a nucleus arrange themselves in a unique geometrical shape, which the author calls a unique nucleus structure. In addition, the unique nucleus structure of all atoms of an element is assumed to be the same. Therefore, all atoms of an element possess the same chemical characteristics and properties. All isotopes have similar chemical properties, but they possess slightly different physical characteristics, which strongly suggests that all isotopes share a similar nucleus structure. Electrons that are revolving around a nucleus pass more frequently when the protons are more saturated; therefore, the unique nucleus structure of an element moulds the shape and size of the unique orbital, which in turn determines the isotope's physical and chemical characteristics.

Any changes to the stockpile of stationary photons on nucleons result in a change in the strength of the angular momentum of those nucleons. Stockpiling photons from the surroundings or dissipating photons to the surroundings either strengthens or weakens the angular momentum of the nucleons involved, which subsequently causes the unique nucleus structure to flex in a certain manner. Flexing of the unique nucleus structure results in a modification of the orbital's shape and size. This in turn leads to modification of the element's chemical characteristics.

Atoms and molecules are constantly exchanging photons with their surroundings. At high ambient temperatures especially, nucleons absorb more photons from the surroundings than they dissipate. On the other hand, at low ambient temperatures, nucleons shed more photons to the surroundings than they absorb. Without any doubt, the unique nucleus structure of an element remains the same at different temperatures, but it does flex to a certain extent according to the intensity of the ambient temperature. Therefore, an equilibrial chemical reaction occurs at a specific rate at different temperatures as the unique nucleus structure flexes to a different extent. So, the different flexure makes the unique nucleus structure possess slightly different chemical and physical characteristics.

There is no doubt that a chemical reaction takes place when the sharing of electrons occurs. The chemical characteristics of an individual component of a compound are altered after undergoing a chemical reaction. For instance, the chemical characteristics of iron atoms are different from the ferrous ions of ferrous oxide. This suggests that the orbital of a component of a compound is altered by a chemical reaction. The unique nucleus structure of a component of a compound remains almost the same as it was before the chemical reaction (i.e. it has a similar unique nucleus structure, but the nucleons are oriented in a slightly different way) except it is now flexed to a different extent, meaning that the size and shape of the orbital has experienced a *slight* alteration. Indirectly, this implies that the so-called chemical energy is harnessed not only from the shared electrons but also from the nuclei of reactants.

How can a unique nucleus structure be flexed? Generally, heat is either absorbed or released during a chemical reaction. Heat is the result of the dissipation of photons. It is the result of a chemical reaction's equal-sum game, where any gained stationary photons must be derived from somewhere or where any lost photons lead to a gain of stationary photons by other elements, which complies with the law of conservation of matter. Both absorption and dissipation of photons to the surroundings, especially when done by the nucleons of an atom, leads to a modification to the strength of their angular momentum. This indirectly proves that photons are particles and that dynamic photons possess momentum, as stationary photons that adhere to nucleons transform a part of their momentum into the form of angular momentum. Another portion of the dynamic photons' energy transforms into magnetic energy. Dynamic photons that adhere to electrons also help top up the electrons' momentum. This takes place especially during the enlargement of the orbital, when more-massive stationary electrons are able to shift their orbitals farther away from nuclei than before. So the heat that dissipates from the electrons, especially when the size of the orbital shrinks after a chemical reaction (which means after the electrons have lost a sizeable number of photons), causes the electrons to orbit much closer to the nucleus. Generally, the size of the orbital only leads us to speculate about the level of saturation of the photons on those electrons. A larger-sized orbital suggests that the electrons are saturated with more photons. A smaller-sized orbital signifies that there are fewer photons on the stationary electrons within the orbital. An orbital may also become enlarged once it captures additional stationary electrons.

Since the size of nucleons is much larger than the size of electrons, nucleons are capable of stockpiling an enormous number of stationary photons or dissipating an abundance of dynamic photons to the surroundings. Any change in the number of stationary photons remaining on nucleons directly affects the nucleons' strength of angular momentum. Therefore, the unique nucleus structure of a component of a compound is slightly different from the nuclear structure of the reactants before the chemical reaction as a result of changes to the stockpile of stationary photons, which leads to modification of the unique nucleus structure. For instance, during an endothermic chemical reaction, heat is absorbed from the surroundings. Just assume that every atom of a compound is absorbing photons from the surroundings. The orbital may also become enlarged as a result, but this is not necessarily true for all endothermic chemical reactions. This indicates that nucleons play a more prominent role than electrons in chemical reactions.

On the other hand, we expect nucleons to dissipate more photons to the surroundings than the electrons dissipate during an exothermic chemical reaction. This is because nucleons have a larger stockpile of stationary photons even if the size of the orbital also experiences shrinkage, which may not necessarily be true for all exothermic chemical reactions. In other words, the orbital of some compounds actually becomes enlarged during an exothermic reaction. Simultaneously, the unique nucleus structure of the atoms remains unchanged, except that the strength of the angular momentum of the nucleons has been altered, which leads the nucleons to flex while they try to maintain the stability of their unique nucleus structure. A slight modification to the unique nucleus structure of atoms leads to simultaneous changes in the size and shape of the atoms' orbital. Thus, the energy content, as well as the chemical characteristics of the atoms of reactants, is different before and after a chemical reaction.

Nucleons are much larger than electrons. Any big chunk of energy that is released or absorbed during a chemical reaction must be contributed by the nucleons of the reactants' nuclei. Obviously, quantum scientists have overlooked the important role that is played by the nuclei of atoms during a chemical reaction.

If the ionic/atomic size of a component of a compound is much larger after a chemical reaction, then the element will not necessarily possess a higher energy content if its nucleus does not contain a larger number of stationary photons after the chemical reaction. Obviously the element's electrons gain more stationary photons after a chemical reaction because the heavier electrons shift farther away from the nucleus; thus, the element's ionic size is larger than it was before the chemical reaction. This might also be because the anion has brought additional stationary electrons into the orbital. Therefore, the ionic size of a component of a compound may not be used as a yardstick to gauge the energy content before or after the chemical reaction. This is because nucleons (which are much larger than electrons, remember) are able to stockpile an abundance of stationary photons, and these too can release a colossal number of dynamic photons into the surroundings. Obviously, a larger orbital and a higher stockpile of stationary photons trapped within the nucleus of a reactant will considerably shrink the element's atomic size and also substantially reduce the nucleus's stockpile of stationary photons, so the element will be perceived as having released a great deal of intense heat during an exothermic reaction.

Both chemical energy and nuclear energy are derived mostly from nuclei. During the release of chemical energy, the unique nucleus structure remains roughly the same as it was before the chemical reaction. On the other hand, the atoms' unique nucleus structure undergoes a restructuring during fission (i.e. the size of the nucleus is reduced to one smaller nucleus or several much smaller nuclei. Undoubtedly, a larger nucleus contains a higher stockpile of stationary photons, so the nucleons have a stronger angular momentum in order to help keep the nucleus cohesive despite the fact that it has more protons within its structure. The presence of more protons results in stronger repulsive forces among protons. In other words, the nucleus of a larger and denser element possesses tremendous excess energy, as nucleons are saturated with an abundance of stationary photons. An enormous number of dynamic photons are released from a nucleus when it fragments into a smaller nucleus or nuclei. A weaker angular momentum is needed to maintain the stability and cohesiveness of those much smaller nuclei).

The atmosphere of the sun contains an abundance of hydrogen and helium, but this does not necessarily validate the fusion theory. All dense radioactive substances were created during the Big Bang. Due to the expansion of the universe, more and more kinetic energy will be transformed into universal gravitational potential energy. The weakening of the angular momentum of the nucleons of dense elements will gradually transform those elements into radioactive substances, which will start to release dynamic photons into the surroundings as a result of radioactivity.

All stars are believed to contain an abundance of dense radioactive substances. When radioactive substances decay, they emit helium nuclei through the process of alpha emission. These helium nuclei eventually become helium atoms. Similarly, either emitted protons or emitted neutrons transform into hydrogen atoms. Therefore, the atmosphere of all stars is enriched with hydrogen gas and helium gas.

The sun releases light and heat as a result of nuclear fission. The construction of heavier nuclei from simpler nuclei requires a greater compaction of stationary photons on the nucleons to boost the strength of their angular momentum so they can overcome the stronger repulsive forces that arise among the additional protons within the nuclei. Instead of releasing energy, the fusion process requires additional energy to compact the nucleons of denser elements and the abundance of stationary photons. Therefore, the fusion process is not a feasible method of deriving energy. This casts doubt on the claim that the sun generates intense energy through fusion.

Without any doubt, all stars generate heat and energy inside their cores through the fission process, which takes place inside the atoms of very dense radioactive substances. The author refuses to believe that there is abundance of hydrogen inside the core of the sun simply because hydrogen is the lightest element. Submitting the unique nucleus structure of a heavy radioactive atom like uranium to the restructuring process normally weakens the nucleons' angular momentum tremendously. This indirectly implies that the new, but simpler and smaller, unique nucleus structures of the daughter atoms are more stable (this is because there is a lighter repulsive electrostatic force among the fewer protons that are present within the nucleus). The weaker angular momentum of the nucleons enables the atom to maintain stability with its new unique nucleus structure. Thus, an abundance of excess photons are released to the surroundings during fission. During the detonation of an atomic bomb, tremendous heat is released to the surroundings. Apparently a large portion of that dissipated heat is derived from nucleons during fission, which is the restructuring of the unique nucleus structure of dense radioactive substances. Nuclear energy (which is tapped from the stockpile of stationary photons on nucleons) is a non-renewable source of energy simply because it is impossible to utilize a reversal process when synthesizing larger nuclei from simpler, lighter nuclei, but these very dense elements were synthesized shortly after the Big Bang explosion when kinetic energy was at its maximum level and when the abundance of dynamic photons and nucleons were saturated within a small, confined area of space at the centre of the universe. In other words, the fusion process could only take place shortly after the Big Bang explosion, when the abundance of nucleons bundled together to form very dense elements. Most likely, not very many nucleons were lucky enough to escape the process of being churned into denser elements to form hydrogen or helium. The increase in the cumulative volume of both hydrogen and helium gases in the atmosphere of both the earth and the sun is the result of the radioactivity of very dense substances inside the earth's core and the sun.

The author strongly believes that a new theory should replace obsolete quantum mechanics in the near future. This is because matter cannot be transformed into energy as dictated by Einstein's $E = mc^2$. The downfall of quantum mechanics is imminent. Statistics will likely share the fate of quantum physics.

The collapse of quantum physics will naturally limit the usefulness of statistics to scientific researchers. Statistics will remain important for redistributing the collected data of an experiment according to the desire of the researcher, but it will now be free of bias and prejudice. In addition, statistics will remain useful for establishing correlations between collected data, and a statistician will be able to reject any bad data (i.e. "bad" in terms of the user's perception; thus, a researcher will strike out the so-called bad data to justify his or her presumption) to arrive at a result that fits with his or her preference and perception. Lastly, like all mathematical manipulations, statistics must maintain its ability to reflect reality and its usefulness in reflecting reality in parallel with the law of conservation of matter and the law of conservation of energy.

Reality and Redistribution

Occasionally, collected data are redistributed according to specific statistical characteristics. Some statistical data such as binomial probabilities, normal curve areas, values of t, values of x^2, the value of $F_{0.05}$ and $F_{0.01}$, critical values of r, and critical values of u are used in redistributing the collected data. Undoubtedly, the redistribution of data has distorted and reshaped the actual distribution. Regardless of the statistical redistribution that is employed, the reality (imperfect hard data) is distorted.

A country's governmental bodies, such as the taxation department and the national registrar department, possess crucial information to help the government make certain decisions regarding infrastructure development, the economy, taxation, and so forth. Normally, governmental bodies don't have to perform statistical assessments because hard data that mirror reality are readily available to them. These hard data provide a big, clear picture. Private companies that don't have access to governmental data have to carry out surveys to get a better picture of what they want to know, or they might have to purchase data from commercial banks or credit card companies to gain insight into one facet of the big picture. Therefore, the accuracy of their data collection hinges on how they poll the data, as well as on the timing of the surveys and where the surveys are conducted. Normally, private companies have preset ideas about the outcome of their assessments. They truncate any data that they perceive to be wrong or bad, at least in their opinion. Then they redistribute the data according to a specific statistical method so that it reflects their anticipated outcome. Any unnecessary distortion to the original distribution of the collected data after the redistribution is likely to be misleading. It also leads to an erroneous outcome after analysis. At best, the redistribution of the hard data should enhance the accuracy of the outcome of the analysis based on the new distribution. Judgement should be exercised when choosing a better statistical characteristic before carrying out a redistribution of the original data so that the redistribution leads to the correct outcome of the analysis. Any skewing of the initial distribution of the hard data does not alter the reality. Instead, the outcome of the analysis after it is transformed by redistribution will likely be distorted and bent. At best, redistribution should enhance the outcome of the analysis so that it aids in understanding the reality.

The categorization of grades for a standardized public examination at both the primary and secondary levels should be based on a normal distribution of the data. Actually, the raw examination results of all primary and secondary students are the true reflection of the students' achievement. To assign fair and equitable grades to students, one must inevitably redistribute the examination grades. The normal distribution is a very good choice for assigning appropriate grades to gauge the students' performance, as the outcome does not look so punishing. At the same time, it serves the purpose of distinguishing students based solely on their performance. Then again, the normal distribution reflects our assumption and bias about the supposed distribution of students' marks for a particular examination, as the majority of the scores cluster near the mean of the scores and the students' actual scores may not necessarily comply with the normal distribution. The basis of the assumption is that a handful of students will earn excellent grades and a small number of students will earn low marks. If a student scores 76 per cent on an examination, then his adjusted mark could be lower or higher than 76 per cent depending on the general performance of the rest of the students in his class – and also depending on what redistribution model the teacher uses in the redistribution of students' scores. The most obvious bias of any redistribution is that the shape of the redistribution is always assumed to be symmetrical and normal, with a smooth curve reflecting all the redistributed data and the highest number of students earning the mean score.

On the other hand, a slightly skewed redistribution may be used for assessing the performance of undergraduate students. This is mainly because all college students must meet minimum requirements before being accepted into a university program. The college students who are considered members of an elite segment of a nation's general population have performed satisfactorily in their academic programs. There are much more stringent entrance requirements for postgraduate programs. This is so that only high achievers are permitted to further their studies in their respective field of interest. Fewer students are likely to be accepted into a postgraduate program because the requirements are more stringent, there is a greater financial burden, they have no interest in a low-paying teaching career, it will take them longer to graduate, and they are not guaranteed to earn a passing grade on their research thesis. In addition, postgraduate students who choose to stay in their program until they graduate are likely be the ones to obtain satisfactory results in their studies and research. Indirectly they also show their keenness for and interest in their field coupled with their strong determination to pursue their postgraduate program. Therefore, the assessment for a postgraduate program is likely to be even more skewed than the assessment for an undergraduate program, as shown in Figure 23. Unlike any redistribution, the original distribution of grades, especially for undergraduate and postgraduate students, is not necessarily symmetrical, as shown in Figure 23.

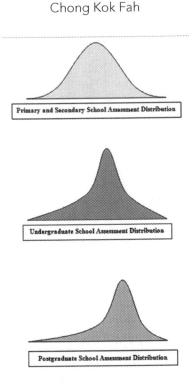

Primary and Secondary School Assessment Distribution

Undergraduate School Assessment Distribution

Postgraduate School Assessment Distribution

Normally, the major purpose for skewing the original distribution is to recategorize all participants so that they meet a specific objective, such as grading the performance of students on a public examination. Unfortunately all statistical redistribution models contort the redistributed data into a symmetrical shape and the redistribution curve is smooth. When the choice is made to redistribute collected data, the redistributed data should reflect reality and also serve the purpose of skewing the original distribution, regardless of which particular statistical redistribution one chooses to use. Reality is reality. Statistics will never be able to bend reality. In addition, no statistical method is good enough to provide an understanding of a real situation if the conditions are manipulated, which would make all the collected data incapable of reflecting reality. Subsequently, wrong conclusions are drawn from the redistributed bad data.

Chapter 6

Matrices

Matrices Have Limited Applications

Matrices are commonly used to find the point of intersection of several first-order equations, provided that those equations are determinate, meaning that the number of unknowns is equal to the number of equations. Take for example the two following first-order equations, each of which has two unknowns. The equations $x + 2y = 5$ and $3x + 2y = 18$ can be expressed in matrix form, as shown below:

$$[\mathbf{a}] \times [\mathbf{b}] = [\mathbf{c}]$$

$$\begin{vmatrix} 1 & 2 \end{vmatrix} \begin{vmatrix} x \end{vmatrix} \quad \begin{vmatrix} 5 \end{vmatrix}$$
$$\qquad\qquad = $$
$$\begin{vmatrix} 3 & 2 \end{vmatrix} \begin{vmatrix} y \end{vmatrix} \quad \begin{vmatrix} 18 \end{vmatrix}$$

Since this matrix problem is determinate, we conclude that the point of intersection of these two linear equations exists. Indirectly, this implies that matrix **a** has an inverse matrix, $\mathbf{a}^{-1}$, and the inverse matrix **a** multiplied by matrix **a** is equal to matrix identity **i**. On the other hand, inverse matrices **a** and $\mathbf{a}^{-1}$ multiplied by matrix **a** equals the point of intersection for the two linear equations, which is the answer that we are seeking.

In conclusion, the problem regarding matrices is that they must have a determinate and that all variables – the independent and dependent variables of all equations involved – must be of the first order; in addition, all involved variables are unit-less or dimensionless. Once all variables have their respective units, all computations of matrices become inoperable because the cumulative units of the computations turn out to be illogical. Such conditions limit the usefulness of matrices and at the same time challenge the validity of the computed outcomes. In short, matrices are mathematical concepts embedded with numerous logic errors that are absolute and should be unlearned.

Appendix

1cm Drawn Radius to Represent Physical 1cm Radius

Area of Quarter of a Circle in term of 2mm×2mm squares $=$ Area of Segment ① to Segment ⑦ in term of 2mm×2mm Squares.

Area of Segment ① $= 4 \times 1$ 2mm×2mm squares $= 4$ 2mm×2mm squares

Area of Segment ② $= \dfrac{1 \times 2}{2}$ 2mm×2mm squares $= 1$ 2mm×2mm Square

Area of Segment ③ $= 2 \times 3$ 2mm×2mm squares $= 6$ 2mm×2mm squares

Area of Segment ④ $= \dfrac{1 \times 1}{2}$ 2mm×2mm squares $= 0.5$ 2mm×2mm square

Area of Segment ⑤ $= \dfrac{1 \times 2}{2}$ 2mm×2mm squares $= 1$ 2mm×2mm square

Area of Segment ⑥ $= 2 \times 1$ 2mm×2mm squares $= 2$ 2mm×2mm squares

Area of Segment ⑦ $= 5 \times 1$ 2mm×2mm squares $= 5$ 2mm×2mm squares

Area of Quarter of a Circle $= (4 + 1 + 6 + 0.5 + 1 + 2 + 5)$ 2mm×2mm Squares

$$= 19.5 \text{ 2mm×2mm squares}$$

Area of a Circle $= 4 \times 19.5$ 2mm×2mm squares

$$= 78 \text{ 2mm×2mm squares}$$

Since $1cm^2 = 5 \times 5$ 2mm×2mm Squares

Area of 1cm Radius of a Circle in cm^2 $= 78 \dfrac{\text{2mm×2mm}}{\text{squares}} \times \dfrac{1cm^2}{25 \text{ 2mm×2mm Squares}}$

$$= 3.12 \ cm^2$$

Assume πR^2 is Correct, Then $\pi (1cm)^2 = \pi \ cm^2$

$\therefore \pi$ is 3.12

2cm Drawn Radius to Represent Physical 1cm Radius

Area of Quarter of a Circle = Area of Segment ① to Segment ⑪
in term of 2mm x 2mm squares in term of 2mm x 2mm squares

Area of Segment ① = 2×10 2mm×2mm squares = 20 2mm×2mm squares

Area of Segment ② = $\frac{1×3}{2}$ 2mm×2mm squares = 1.5 2mm×2mm squares

Area of Segment ③ = $\frac{1×1}{2}$ 2mm×2mm squares = 0.5 2mm×2mm square

Area of Segment ④ = $\frac{2×2}{2}$ 2mm×2mm squares = 2 2mm×2mm squares

Area of Segment ⑤ = $\frac{1×1}{2}$ 2mm×2mm squares = 0.5 2mm×2mm squares

Area of Segment ⑥ = $\frac{1×3}{2}$ 2mm×2mm squares = 1.5 2mm×2mm squares

Area of Segment ⑦ = 7×3 2mm×2mm squares = 21 2mm×2mm squares

Area of Segment ⑧ = 2×8 2mm×2mm squares = 16 2mm×2mm squares

Area of Segment ⑨ = 1×6 2mm×2mm squares = 6 2mm×2mm squares

Area of Segment ⑩ = 2×4 2mm×2mm squares = 8 2mm×2mm squares

Area of Segment ⑪ = 1×3 2mm×2mm squares = 3 2mm×2mm squares

Area of Quarter of a Circle = (20 + 1.5 + 0.5 + 2 + 0.5 + 1.5 + 21 + 16 + 6 + 8 + 3) 2mm×2mm squares

= 80 2mm×2mm squares

Area of a Circle = 4×80 2mm×2mm squares

= 320 2mm×2mm squares

Since $1 cm^2 = 10 \times 10$ 2mm×2mm Squares

Area of a Circle $= 320$ 2mm×2mm squares $\times \dfrac{1 cm^2}{100 \text{ 2mm×2mm squares}}$
in cm^2

$\qquad\qquad\quad = 3.2 cm^2$

Assume πR^2 is correct, the $\pi (1 cm)^2 = \pi cm^2$

$\therefore \quad \pi$ is 3.2

111

3cm Drawn Radius to Represent Physical 1cm Radius

Area of quarter of a Circle = Area of Segment ① to Segment ⑭
in term of 2mm×2mm squares   in term of 2mm×2mm squares

Area of Segment ① = 2×15 2mm×2mm squares = 30 2mm×2mm squares

Area of Segment ② = $\frac{1 \times 3}{2}$ 2mm×2mm squares = 1.5 2mm×2mm squares

Area of Segment ③ = $\frac{1 \times 2.5}{2}$ 2mm×2mm squares = 1.25 2mm×2mm squares

Area of Segment ④ = $\frac{2 \times 2.5}{2}$ 2mm×2mm squares = 2.5 2mm×2mm squares

Area of Segment ⑤ = $\frac{1 \times 1}{2}$ 2mm×2mm squares = 0.5 2mm×2mm squares

Area of Segment ⑥ = $\frac{2 \times 2.5}{2}$ 2mm×2mm squares = 2.5 2mm×2mm squares

Area of Segment ⑦ = $\frac{1 \times 2.5}{2}$ 2mm×2mm squares = 1.25 2mm×2mm squares

Area of Segment ⑧ = $\frac{1 \times 3}{2}$ 2mm×2mm squares = 1.5 2mm×2mm squares

Area of Segment ⑨ = 3×12 2mm×2mm squares = 36 2mm×2mm squares

Area of Segment ⑩ = 2.5×11 2mm×2mm squares = 27.5 2mm×2mm squares

Area of Segment ⑪ = 2.5×9 2mm×2mm squares = 22.5 2mm×2mm squares

Area of Segment ⑫ = 1×8 2mm×2mm squares = 8 2mm×2mm squares

Area of Segment ⑬ = 2×5.5 2mm×2mm squares = 11 2mm×2mm squares

Area of Segment ⑭ = 1×3 2mm×2mm squares = 3 2mm×2mm squares

Area of Segment ⑮ $= 2 \times 13$ 2mm×2mm Squares $= 26$ 2mm×2mm Squares

Area of Quarter of a Circle $= (30 + 1.5 + 1.25 + 2.5 + 0.5 + 2.5 + 1.25 + 1.5 +$
$$36 + 27.5 + 22.5 + 8 + 11 + 3 + 26)$$
2mm×2mm Squares
$$= 175 \text{ 2mm×2mm squares}$$

Area of a Circle $= 4 \times 175$ 2mm×2mm squares
$$= 700 \text{ 2mm×2mm squares}$$

Since $1 cm^2 = 15 \times 15$ 2mm×2mm squares

Area of 1cm Radius of a Circle $= 700$ 2mm×2mm $\times \dfrac{1 cm^2}{225 \text{ 2mm×2mm squares}}$
in cm^2 squares
$$= 3.11111111 \ cm^2$$

Assume πR^2 is correct, then $\pi (1cm)^2 = \pi \ cm^2$

∴ π is 3.11111111

4 cm Drawn Radius to Represent Physical 1 cm Radius

Area of Quarter of a Circle
in term of 2mm×2mm squares
= Area of Segment ① to Segment ⑰
in term of 2mm×2mm squares

Area of Segment ① = 2×20 2mm×2mm squares = 40 2mm×2mm squares

Area of Segment ② = $\frac{1×4}{2}$ 2mm×2mm squares = 2 2mm×2mm squares

Area of Segment ③ = $\frac{1×2.5}{2}$ 2mm×2mm squares = 1.25 2mm×2mm squares

Area of Segment ④ = $\frac{2×3.5}{2}$ 2mm×2mm squares = 3.5 2mm×2mm squares

Area of Segment ⑤ = $\frac{2×2}{2}$ 2mm×2mm squares = 2 2mm×2mm squares

Area of Segment ⑥ = $\frac{2×2}{2}$ 2mm×2mm squares = 2 2mm×2mm squares

Area of Segment ⑦ = $\frac{2×3.5}{2}$ 2mm×2mm squares = 3.5 2mm×2mm squares

Area of Segment ⑧ = $\frac{1×2.5}{2}$ 2mm×2mm squares = 1.25 2mm×2mm squares

Area of Segment ⑨ = $\frac{1×4}{2}$ 2mm×2mm squares = 2 2mm×2mm squares

Area of Segment ⑩ = 4×17 2mm×2mm squares = 68 2mm×2mm squares

Area of Segment ⑪ = 2.5×16 2mm×2mm squares = 40 2mm×2mm squares

Area of Segment ⑫ = 3.5×14 2mm×2mm squares = 49 2mm×2mm squares

Area of Segment ⑬ = 2×12 2mm×2mm squares = 24 2mm×2mm squares

Area of Segment ⑭ = 2×10 2mm×2mm squares = 20 2mm×2mm squares

Area of Segment ⑮ $= 2 \times 6.5$ 2mm$\times$2mm squares $= 13$ 2mm$\times$2mm squares

Area of Segment ⑯ $= 1 \times 4$ 2mm$\times$2mm squares $= 4$ 2mm$\times$2mm squares

Area of Segment ⑰ $= 2 \times 18$ 2mm$\times$2mm squares $= 36$ 2mm$\times$2mm squares

Area of Quarter of a Circle $= (40 + 2 + 1.25 + 3.5 + 2 + 2 + 3.5 + 1.25 + 2 +$
$$68 + 40 + 49 + 24 + 20 + 13 + 4 + 36)$$
2mm$\times$2mm squares
$$= 311.5 \text{ 2mm} \times \text{2mm squares}$$

Area of a circle $= 4 \times 311.5$ 2mm$\times$2mm squares
$$= 1246 \text{ 2mm} \times \text{2mm squares}$$

Since $1 cm^2 = 20 \times 20$ 2mm$\times$2mm squares

Area of 1cm Radius of a circle $= 1246$ 2mm$\times$2mm squares $\times \dfrac{1 cm^2}{400 \text{ 2mm}\times\text{2mm squares}}$
in cm^2
$$= 3.115 \ cm^2$$

Assume πR^2 is correct, then $\pi (1cm)^2 = \pi \ cm^2$

$\therefore$ π is 3.115

5 cm Drawn Radius to Represent Physical 1cm Radius

Area of Quarter of a Circle = Area of Segment ① to Segment ⑬
in term of 2mm × 2mm squares   in term of 2mm × 2mm squares

Area of Segment ① = 2×25 2mm×2mm squares = 50 2mm×2mm squares

Area of Segment ② = $\frac{1×5}{2}$ 2mm×2mm squares = 2.5 2mm×2mm squares

Area of Segment ③ = $\frac{1×2.5}{2}$ 2mm×2mm squares = 1.25 2mm×2mm squares

Area of Segment ④ = $\frac{1×2.5}{2}$ 2mm×2mm squares = 1.25 2mm×2mm squares

Area of Segment ⑤ = $\frac{2×3}{2}$ 2mm×2mm squares = 3 2mm×2mm squares

Area of Segment ⑥ = $\frac{2×2}{2}$ 2mm×2mm squares = 2 2mm×2mm squares

Area of Segment ⑦ = $\frac{1×1}{2}$ 2mm×2mm squares = 0.5 2mm×2mm squares

Area of Segment ⑧ = $\frac{2×2}{2}$ 2mm×2mm squares = 2 2mm×2mm squares

Area of Segment ⑨ = $\frac{2×3}{2}$ 2mm×2mm squares = 3 2mm×2mm squares

Area of Segment ⑩ = $\frac{1×2.5}{2}$ 2mm×2mm squares = 1.25 2mm×2mm squares

Area of Segment ⑪ = $\frac{1×2.5}{2}$ 2mm×2mm squares = 1.25 2mm×2mm squares

Area of Segment ⑫ = $\frac{1×5}{2}$ 2mm×2mm squares = 2.5 2mm×2mm squares

Area of Segment ⑬ = 5×22 2mm×2mm squares = 110 2mm×2mm squares

116

Area of Segment ⑭ $= 2.5 \times 21$ 2mm×2mm squares $= 52.5$ 2mm × 2mm squares

Area of Segment ⑮ $= 2.5 \times 20$ 2mm×2mm squares $= 50$ 2mm×2mm squares

Area of Segment ⑯ $= 3 \times 18$ 2mm×2mm squares $= 54$ 2mm×2mm squares

Area of Segment ⑰ $= 2 \times 16$ 2mm×2mm squares $= 32$ 2mm×2mm squares

Area of Segment ⑱ $= 1 \times 15$ 2mm×2mm squares $= 15$ 2mm×2mm squares

Area of Segment ⑲ $= 2 \times 13$ 2mm×2mm squares $= 26$ 2mm×2mm squares

Area of Segment ⑳ $= 2 \times 10$ 2mm×2mm squares $= 20$ 2mm×2mm squares

Area of Segment ㉑ $= 1 \times 7.5$ 2mm×2mm squares $= 7.5$ 2mm×2mm squares

Area of Segment ㉒ $= 1 \times 5$ 2mm×2mm squares $= 5$ 2mm×2mm squares

Area of Segment ㉓ $= 2 \times 23$ 2mm×2mm squares $= 46$ 2mm×2mm squares.

Area of Quarter of a Circle $= (50 + 2.5 + 1.25 + 1.25 + 3 + 2 + 0.5 + 2 + 3 + 1.25$
$+ 1.25 + 2.5 + 110 + 52.5 + 50 + 54 + 32 + 15 + 26$
$+ 20 + 7.5 + 5 + 46)$ 2mm×2mm squares
$= 488.5$ 2mm×2mm squares

Area of a Circle $= 4 \times 488.5$ 2mm×2mm squares
$= 1954$ 2mm×2mm squares

Since $1cm^2 = 25 \times 25$ 2mm×2mm squares

Area of 1cm Radius of a circle in cm^2 $= 1954$ 2mm×2mm squares $\times \dfrac{1 cm^2}{625 \ 2mm \times 2mm \ squares}$

$= 3.1264 \ cm^2$

Assume πR^2 is correct, then $\pi(1cm)^2 = \pi cm^2$

$\therefore \pi$ is 3.1264

117

6 cm Drawn Radius to Represent Physical 1cm Radius

Area of Quarter of a Circle _____ = Area of Segment ① ... Segment ⑫
in term of 2mm × 2mm squares = in terms of 2mm × 2mm squares

Area of Segment ① = 30 × 2 2mm × 2mm squares = 60 2mm × 2mm squares

Area of Segment ② = 1.5 × 5.5 2mm × 2mm squares = 8.75 2mm × 2mm squares

Area of Segment ③ = 2.5 × 5.5 2mm × 2mm squares = 5.5 2mm × 2mm squares

Area of Segment ④ = 1 × 5 2mm × 2mm squares = 1 2mm × 2mm squares

Area of Segment ⑤ = 2 × 1 2mm × 2mm squares = 2 2mm × 2mm squares

Area of Segment ⑥ = 2 × 3.5 2mm × 2mm squares = 7.5 2mm × 2mm squares

Area of Segment ⑦ = 1.5 × 1.5 2mm × 2mm squares = 1.125 2mm × 2mm squares

Area of Segment ⑧ = 2 × 5.5 2mm × 2mm squares = 2.5 2mm × 2mm squares

Area of Segment ⑨ = 2 × 1 2mm × 2mm squares = 3 2mm × 2mm squares

Area of Segment ⑩ = 1 × 2 2mm × 2mm squares = 1 2mm × 2mm squares

Area of Segment ⑪ = 2 × 5.5 2mm × 2mm squares = 5.5 2mm × 2mm squares

Area of Segment ⑫ = 1 × 5.5 2mm × 2mm squares = 2.75 2mm × 2mm squares

Area of Segment (13) = 1x2 2mmx2mm squares = 2 2mmx2mm squares.

Area of Segment (14) = 5.5x29 2mmx2mm squares = 159.5 2mmx2mm squares

Area of Segment (15) = 5.5x27 2mmx2mm squares = 148.5 2mmx2mm squares

Area of Segment (16) = 2x26 2mmx2mm squares = 52 2mmx2mm squares

Area of Segment (17) = 3x24 2mmx2mm squares = 72 2mmx2mm squares.

Area of Segment (18) = 2.5x22 2mmx2mm squares = 55 2mmx2mm squares

Area of Segment (19) = 1.5x20.5 2mmx2mm squares = 30.75 2mmx2mm squares.

Area of Segment (20) = 2x18 2mmx2mm squares = 36 2mmx2mm squares

Area of Segment (21) = 2x15 2mmx2mm squares = 30 2mmx2mm squares

Area of Segment (22) = 1x13 2mmx2mm squares = 13 2mmx2mm squares.

Area of Segment (23) = 2x7.5 2mmx2mm squares = 15 2mmx2mm squares.

Area of Quarter of a Circle = (60 + 2.75 + 5.5 + 1 + 3 + 2.5 + 1.125 + 2.5 + 3 + 1 + 5.5 + 2.75 + 2 + 159.5 + 148.5 + 52 + 72 + 55 + 30.75 + 36 + 30 + 13 + 15) 2mmx2mm squares

= 704.375 2mmx2mm squares

Area of a Circle = 4 x 704.375 2mmx2mm squares

= 2817.5 2mmx2mm squares

Since $1cm^2$ = 30x30 2mmx2mm squares

Area of 1cm Radius of a Circle in cm^2 = 2817.5 2mmx2mm squares x $\frac{1cm^2}{900 \text{ 2mmx2mm squares}}$

= $3.130555556 \ cm^2$

Page 11/19

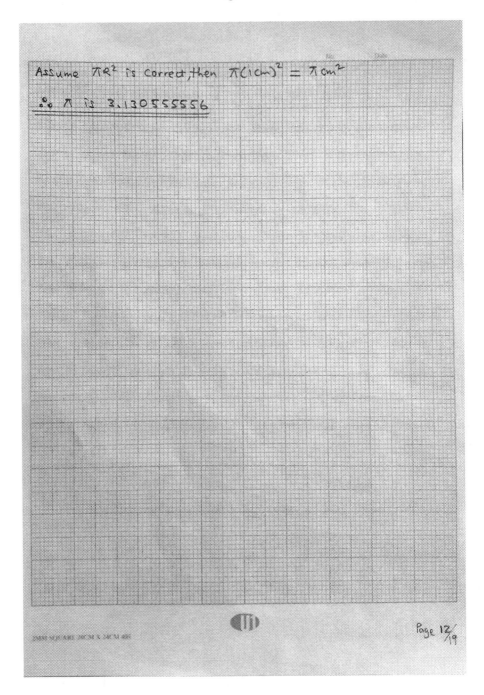

Assume πR^2 is correct, then $\pi(1cm)^2 = \pi\,cm^2$

$\therefore \pi$ is 3.130555556

120

7cm Drawn Radius to Represent Physical 1cm Radius

Area of Quarter of a Circle in term of 2mm x 2mm squares = Area of Segment ① to Segment ㉗ in term of 2mm x 2mm squares

Area of Segment ① $= 3 \times 35$ 2mm x 2mm squares $= 105$ 2mm x 2mm squares

Area of Segment ② $= \frac{1 \times 5.5}{2}$ 2mm x 2mm squares $= 2.75$ 2mm x 2mm squares

Area of Segment ③ $= \frac{1 \times 3.5}{2}$ 2mm x 2mm squares $= 1.75$ 2mm x 2mm squares

Area of Segment ④ $= \frac{2 \times 4.5}{2}$ 2mm x 2mm squares $= 4.5$ 2mm x 2mm squares

Area of Segment ⑤ $= \frac{2 \times 3}{2}$ 2mm x 2mm squares $= 3$ 2mm x 2mm squares

Area of Segment ⑥ $= \frac{1 \times 1.5}{2}$ 2mm x 2mm squares $= 0.75$ 2mm x 2mm squares

Area of Segment ⑦ $= \frac{2 \times 2.5}{2}$ 2mm x 2mm squares $= 2.5$ 2mm x 2mm squares

Area of Segment ⑧ $= \frac{2.5 \times 2.5}{2}$ 2mm x 2mm squares $= 3.125$ 2mm x 2mm squares

Area of Segment ⑨ $= \frac{2 \times 2.5}{2}$ 2mm x 2mm squares $= 2.5$ 2mm x 2mm squares

Area of Segment ⑩ $= \frac{1 \times 1.5}{2}$ 2mm x 2mm squares $= 0.75$ 2mm x 2mm squares

Area of Segment ⑪ $= \frac{2 \times 3}{2}$ 2mm x 2mm squares $= 3$ 2mm x 2mm squares

Area of Segment ⑫ $= \frac{2 \times 4.5}{2}$ 2mm x 2mm squares $= 4.5$ 2mm x 2mm squares

Page 13/19

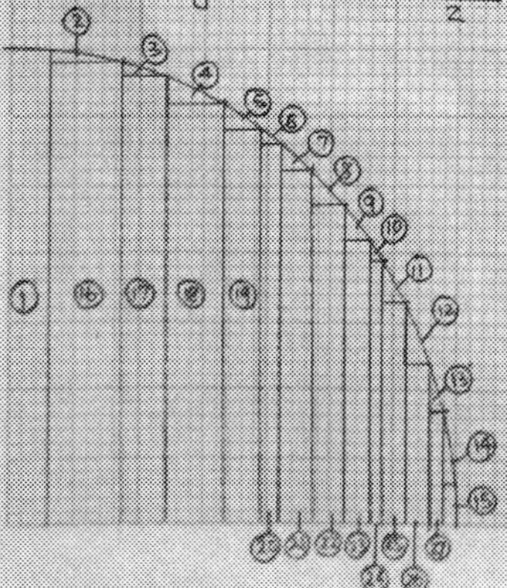

Area of Segment ⑤ = $\frac{1+3.5}{2}$ 2mm×2mm squares = 1.75 2mm×2mm squares

Area of Segment ⑥ = $\frac{1+5.5}{2}$ 2mm×2mm squares = 2.75 2mm×2mm squares

Area of Segment ⑦ = 1×3 2mm×2mm squares = 3 2mm×2mm squares

Area of Segment ⑧ = 5.5×34 2mm×2mm squares = 187 2mm×2mm squares

Area of Segment ⑨ = 3.5×33 2mm×2mm squares = 115.5 2mm×2mm squares

Area of Segment ⑩ = 4.5×31 2mm×2mm squares = 139.5 2mm×2mm squares

Area of Segment ⑪ = 3×29 2mm×2mm squares = 87 2mm×2mm squares

Area of Segment ⑫ = 1.5×28 2mm×2mm squares = 42 2mm×2mm squares

Area of Segment ⑬ = 2.5×26 2mm×2mm squares = 65 2mm×2mm squares

Area of Segment ⑭ = 2.5×23.5 2mm×2mm squares = 58.75 2mm×2mm squares

Area of Segment ⑮ = 2×21 2mm×2mm squares = 42 2mm×2mm squares

Area of Segment ⑯ = 1×19.5 2mm×2mm squares = 19.5 2mm×2mm squares

Area of Segment ⑰ = 2×16.5 2mm×2mm squares = 33 2mm×2mm squares

Area of Segment ⑱ = 2×12 2mm×2mm squares = 24 2mm×2mm squares

Area of Segment ⑲ = 1×8.5 2mm×2mm squares = 8.5 2mm×2mm squares

Area of Quarter of a Circle = (1.75 + 2.75 + 1.75 + 4.5 + 3 + 0.75 + 2.5 + 8.125 +

2.5 + 0.75 + 3 + 4.5 + 1.75 + 2.75 + 3 + 187 + 115.5 +

139.5 + 87 + 42 + 65 + 58.75 + 42 + 19.5 + 33 + 24 +

8.5) 2mm×2mm squares

= 963.375 2mm×2mm squares

Area of a Circle $= 4 \times 963.375$ 2mm×2mm squares

$= 3853.5$ 2mm×2mm squares

Since $1cm^2 = 35 \times 35$ 2mm×2mm squares

Area of 1cm Radius of a Circle in cm^2 $= 3853.5$ 2mm×2mm squares $\times \dfrac{1cm^2}{1225 \text{ 2mm×2mm squares}}$

$= 3.145714286\ cm^2$

Assume πR^2 is correct, then $\pi(1cm)^2 = \pi\ cm^2$

$\therefore$ π is 3.145714286

Page 15/19

8 cm Drawn Radius to Represent 1cm Radius

Area of Quarter of a Circle
in term of 2mm×2mm squares = Area of Segment ① to Segment ㉟
in term of 2mm×2mm squares

Area of Segment ① = 3×40 2mm×2mm squares = 120 2mm×2mm squares

Area of Segment ② = $\frac{1×6.5}{2}$ 2mm×2mm squares = 3.25 2mm×2mm squares

Area of Segment ③ = $\frac{1×3.5}{2}$ 2mm×2mm squares = 1.75 2mm×2mm squares

Area of Segment ④ = $\frac{1×2}{2}$ 2mm×2mm squares = 1 2mm×2mm squares.

Area of Segment ⑤ = $\frac{1×2.5}{2}$ 2mm×2mm squares = 1.25 2mm×2mm squares

Area of Segment ⑥ = $\frac{2×3.5}{2}$ 2mm×2mm squares = 3.5 2mm×2mm squares

Area of Segment ⑦ = $\frac{2×3}{2}$ 2mm×2mm squares = 3 2mm×2mm squares

Area of Segment ⑧ = $\frac{2×2.5}{2}$ 2mm×2mm squares = 2.5 2mm×2mm squares

Area of Segment ⑨ = $\frac{1.5×1.5}{2}$ 2mm×2mm squares = 1.125 2mm×2mm squares

Area of Segment ⑩ = $\frac{0.5×0.5}{2}$ 2mm×2mm squares = 0.125 2mm×2mm squares

Area of Segment ⑪ = $\frac{1.5×1.5}{2}$ 2mm×2mm squares = 1.125 2mm×2mm squares

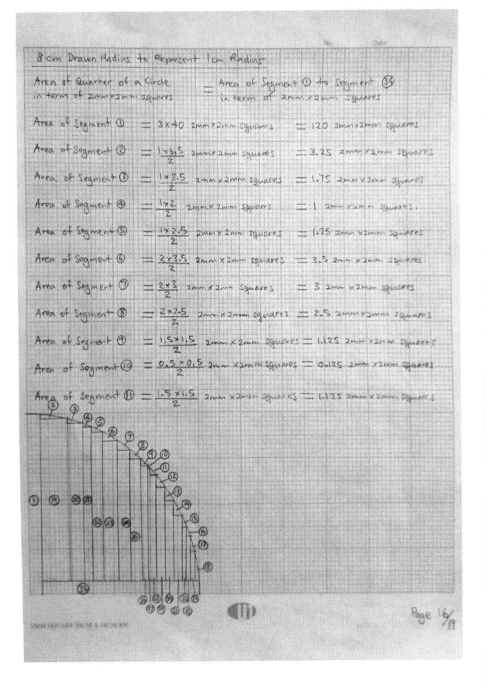

124

Area of Segment ⑫ $= \frac{2 \times 2.5}{2}$ 2mm×2mm squares $= 2.5$ 2mm×2mm squares

Area of Segment ⑬ $= \frac{2 \times 3}{2}$ 2mm×2mm squares $= 3$ 2mm×2mm squares

Area of Segment ⑭ $= \frac{2 \times 3.5}{2}$ 2mm×2mm squares $= 3.5$ 2mm×2mm squares

Area of Segment ⑮ $= \frac{1 \times 2.5}{2}$ 2mm×2mm squares $= 1.25$ 2mm×2mm squares

Area of Segment ⑯ $= \frac{1 \times 2}{2}$ 2mm×2mm squares $= 1$ 2mm×2mm squares

Area of Segment ⑰ $= \frac{1 \times 3.5}{2}$ 2mm×2mm squares $= 1.75$ 2mm×2mm squares

Area of Segment ⑱ $= \frac{1 \times 6.5}{2}$ 2mm×2mm squares $= 3.25$ 2mm×2mm squares

Area of Segment ⑲ $= 6.5 \times 36$ 2mm×2mm squares $= 234$ 2mm×2mm squares

Area of Segment ⑳ $= 3.5 \times 35$ 2mm×2mm squares $= 122.5$ 2mm×2mm squares

Area of Segment ㉑ $= 2 \times 34$ 2mm×2mm squares $= 68$ 2mm×2mm squares

Area of Segment ㉒ $= 2.5 \times 33$ 2mm×2mm squares $= 82.5$ 2mm×2mm squares

Area of Segment ㉓ $= 3.5 \times 31$ 2mm×2mm squares $= 108.5$ 2mm×2mm squares

Area of Segment ㉔ $= 3 \times 29$ 2mm×2mm squares $= 87$ 2mm×2mm squares

Area of Segment ㉕ $= 2.5 \times 27$ 2mm×2mm squares $= 67.5$ 2mm×2mm squares

Area of Segment ㉖ $= 1.5 \times 25.5$ 2mm×2mm squares $= 38.25$ 2mm×2mm squares

Area of Segment ㉗ $= 0.5 \times 25$ 2mm×2mm squares $= 12.5$ 2mm×2mm squares

Area of Segment ㉘ $= 1.5 \times 23.5$ 2mm×2mm squares $= 35.25$ 2mm×2mm squares

Area of Segment ㉙ $= 2 \times 21$ 2mm×2mm squares $= 42$ 2mm×2mm squares

Area of Segment ㉚ $= 2 \times 18$ 2mm×2mm squares $= 36$ 2mm×2mm squares

Area of Segment ㉛ $= 2 \times 14.5$ 2mm×2mm squares $= 29$ 2mm×2mm squares

Area of Segment ㉜ $= 1 \times 12$ 2mm $\times$ 2mm squares $= 12$ 2mm $\times$ 2mm squares

Area of Segment ㉝ $= 1 \times 10$ 2mm $\times$ 2mm squares $= 10$ 2mm $\times$ 2mm squares

Area of Segment ㉞ $= 1 \times 6.5$ 2mm $\times$ 2mm squares $= 6.5$ 2mm $\times$ 2mm squares

Area of Segment ㉟ $= 3 \times 37$ 2mm $\times$ 2mm squares $= 111$ 2mm $\times$ 2mm squares

Area of Quarter of a Circle $= (120 + 3.25 + 1.75 + 1 + 1.25 + 3.5 + 3 + 2.5 + 1.125 +$
$0.125 + 1.125 + 2.5 + 3 + 3.5 + 1.75 + 1 + 1.75 + 3.25 +$
$234 + 122.5 + 68 + 82.5 + 108.5 + 87 + 67.5 + 38.25 +$
$12.5 + 35.25 + 42 + 36 + 29 + 12 + 10 + 6.5 + 111)$
2mm $\times$ 2mm squares
$= 1257.375$ 2mm $\times$ 2mm squares

Area of a Circle $= 4 \times 1257.375$ 2mm $\times$ 2mm squares
$= 5029.5$ 2mm $\times$ 2mm squares

Since 1cm^2 $= 40 \times 40$ 2mm $\times$ 2mm squares

Area of 1cm Radius of a Circle $= 5029.5$ 2mm $\times$ 2mm squares $\times \dfrac{1\text{cm}^2}{1600 \text{ 2mm} \times \text{2mm squares}}$

$= 3.1434375$

Assume πR^2 is correct, then $\pi (1\text{cm})^2 = \pi \text{cm}^2$

$\therefore \pi$ is 3.1434375

Result Summary

Scale Actual : Drawing	Area 1cm² : # of 2mm×2mm Squares	Area of Quarter of a Circle in term of # of 2mm×2mm squares	Area of a Circle in term of # of 2mm× 2mm squares	Area of 1cm Radius of a Circle in term of Cm² *
1cm : 1cm	1cm² : 5×5 2mm×2mm Squares	19.5	78	3.12
1cm : 2cm	1cm² : 10×10 2mm×2mm Squares	80	320	3.2
1cm : 3cm	1cm² : 15×15 2mm×2mm Squares	175	700	3.11111111
1cm : 4cm	1cm² : 20×20 2mm×2mm squares	311.5	1246	3.115
1cm : 5cm	1cm² : 25×25 2mm×2mm Squares	488.5	1954	3.1264
1cm : 6cm	1cm² : 30×30 2mm×2mm squares	704.375	2817.5	3.130555556
1cm : 7cm	1cm² : 35×35 2mm×2mm Squares	963.375	3853.5	3.145714286
1cm : 8cm	1cm² : 40×40 2mm×2mm squares	1257.375	5029.5	3.1484375

* Assume πR^2 is correct in find the area of a circle, then $\pi(1cm)^2$ is equaled to πcm^2. Therefore the area of 1cm Radius of a circle is also equaled the value of π.

Printed in the United States
By Bookmasters